Nymphenburg
Palace, Park and Pavilions

Official guide

Revised by
Gerhard Hojer, Elmar D. Schmid
and Max Tillmann

With additional material by
Ernst Götz

Bayerische
Schlösserverwaltung

Contents

Cover picture: Nymphenburg Palace from the garden side with the central canal

Triton child riding on a dolphin, fountain figure by Guillielmus de Grof, 1722, Badenburg, Great Hall

History

The central building of Nymphenburg from the town side

Previous double page: Aerial view of Nymphenburg Palace and Park from the town side

Nymphenburg Palace, around a two-hour journey to the west of their residential capital, Munich, was the Bavarian rulers' favourite summer residence. This palace complex is of rather unusual design, with separate cube-shaped pavilions elegantly arranged around a central pavilion – which is also in the form of a cube. On the town side is a spacious cour d'honneur bordered by building tracts and a crescent (Rondell), and on the other side is an extensive park.

The complex was not all created at once. The foundation stone was laid in 1664, but the planning, building and conversion continued well into the 19th century. Five rulers from the House of Wittelsbach contributed to the creation of Nymphenburg: the electors Ferdinand Maria, Max Emanuel, Karl Albrecht, Max III Joseph and Max IV Joseph, who became king in 1806 (see short biographies).

THE FOUNDING OF NYMPHENBURG

The palace was begun by Elector Ferdinand Maria, (reigned 1651–1679), who presented his consort Henriette Adelaide of Savoy with Kemnath, a farm purchased on 1.7.1663 for 10,000 florins. The present marked the birth of the heir Max Emanuel a year before. A few days later the electress was already writing to her mother in Turin that she intended to have something built in "Kemmertin" (the court property [Hofmark] of Kemnath); she rejected the plans of the Turin architect Amadeus Castellamonte as too modest and eventually decided in favour of a design by Agostino Barelli of Bologna, who also started building the

Munich Theatinerkirche, likewise in honour of the birth of the young heir. In 1664 the ground was prepared for the palace, but building was slow to start, as up until 1670 a large amount of the available money was tied up in the work on the electress's apartment in the Munich Residence. In 1672 the central building was finally roofed.

Previous double page: Nymphenburg Palace from the town side, in the foreground the basin with the fountain in the palace crescent

For a long time our idea of what Henriette Adelaide's palace looked like was based on an engraving by Michael Wening from 1701, which shows the building as a detached, cube-shaped block in the style of the "villa suburbana" that was common in Upper Italy (p. 11). The façade is of simple design with the five storeys separated by string courses. More recent research, however, has shown that Wening's palace was already the result of a change in the design and subsequent rebuilding (Bauer-Wild, 1986 und 1998). The building invoices preserved from this time show that, right from start, the palace was designed with three wings, a central building and two adjacent pavilions, the form in which it was subsequently completed under Max Emanuel. Since Adelaide expressly requested a spacious property with room for a total of four princely apartments, which in the Nymphenburg building could only be accommodated on the main floor, it was necessary to add extensions. The sources record that in 1674 two relatively large square side pavilions were begun. Construction was now also speeded up, as in 1673 the project had been taken over by a forceful new architect, Henrico Zuccalli from Grisons in Switzerland. He first completed the vaulted ceiling over the Great Hall and in 1674 began the double flight of steps on the town side. He also embarked on major alterations. These primarily involved Barelli's gables and roof extensions, which by then had gone out of fashion; Zuccalli had them taken down again in 1678 and replaced by the present shallow hip roof. The shell of the northern pavilion was completed by 1680. However, in the same year the building work, which had been continued after the death of the electress in 1676, came to a complete stop. The new elector, Max Emanuel, so disliked the design of his mother's palace that he ordered the recently constructed side pavilions to be pulled down altogether. He used the building material for his first palace in Lustheim, which was erected in 1684–1686.

Nymphenburg Palace, copper engraving by Michael Wening, 1701

It has thus been ascertained that the earliest palace complex in Nymphenburg already consisted of several separate buildings. These were also joined by low galleries, which enabled the princely apartments to be spread over several buildings. Contrary to previous opinion, the original Nymphenburg design was neither French nor Dutch in origin, but was based on Turin architecture of the mid-17th century. The concept of linking up a series of separate buildings by means of galleries to create an extensive complex was familiar to Henriette Adelaide from the palace architecture of her home country.

The ground plan on the main floor of the central building was basically as it is today. A suite of four magnificent rooms for the elector was located opposite a symmetrical suite for the electress. The centre of the complex was the Great Hall ("Steinerner Saal"), which already had the dimensions of the present hall. On its west side, however, it was separated by a wall from a smaller adjacent garden hall. The Great Hall initially had smooth, plain walls with magnificent stucco marble portals as ornamental features. In 1675–1676 the vaulted ceiling of the hall was richly decorated with stucco-work, probably by Prospero Breni, which

The electoral couple Ferdinand Maria and Henriette Adelaide, Sebastiano Bombelli, 1666, main palace (Room 11)

was however removed when the hall was renovated in 1755. The stucco marble specialist Andreas Römer and the ornamental carvers Georg Wohlgemuth and Hans Indauer worked from 1673 on the magnificent interior of the two main apartments. In 1676 Römer submitted an estimate for the "guilding of the partly completed and partly begun" ceilings. Paintings with figures were produced for the ceilings by the Italian artists Antonio Domenico Triva, Antonio Zanchi and Stefano Catani and the Swiss artist Joseph Werner, but not all of them were initially installed.

HENRIETTE ADELAIDE OF SAVOY (1636–1676)

The sensuous Munich Baroque culture first began to develop under the influence of a princess: Henriette Adelaide of Savoy. The Italian-born princess grew up in the splendid surroundings of the Turin court. In 1652 she was married at the age of sixteen to Elector Ferdinand Maria of Bavaria (1636–1679), who was the same age. The change from the urbane cultural sphere of her homeland to a country marked by the Thirty Years' War came as a shock to Adelaide. She was also disappointed by her husband's lack of independence. The first years of the marriage were full of conflict, caused in particular by the pro-French attitude of the self-confident princess. The crisis came to a head in 1657, when Ferdinand Maria turned down the imperial title, offered to him by the electors and France, out of consideration for the interests of Vienna. After the birth of the electoral heir in 1662, however, Adelaide had more influence, and was for example instrumental in the conclusion of the Bavarian-French alliance treaty of 1670. Henriette Adelaide's most important legacy is the Baroque culture modelled on the art of Italy and France that she introduced at the Bavarian court. The south apartment of the central building is decorated with works by her gifted court painters.

Previous page: Electress Henriette Adelaide, Jean Delamonce, c. 1674, Munich Residence

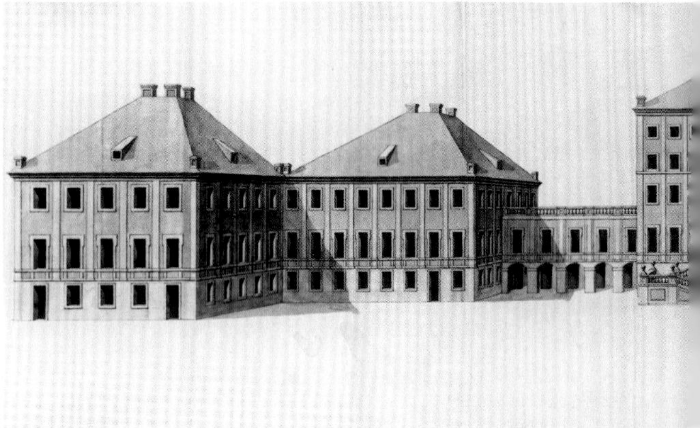

At the same time as the palace was being built, a garden was laid out on the west side. Wening's engraving idealizes not only the architecture, but also the garden, which in 1701 had already been abandoned for 20 years. In the middle of the garden there was originally a small brick garden temple, and from its foundations Wening probably thought this had been a pool. Four fountains which were grouped around the circular building were connected with one another by radiating paths. In the parterre the Bavarian coat of arms and parallel to this probably the Savoyan coat of arms were planted in miniature box trees. A semicircular wall with statue niches separated the garden from the open countryside beyond.

MAX EMANUEL AND NYMPHENBURG, 1680–1726

FIRST BUILDING PERIOD UNDER MAX EMANUEL

It was only in 1701, after his return from the Spanish Netherlands, that Max Emanuel began to take an interest in Nymphenburg. The elector, who had used stone from the incomplete palace as building material for his new project in Lustheim, now saw his mother's legacy with new eyes and

Nymphenburg Palace seen from the east, plan by Henrico Zuccalli, c. 1702, Paris, Bibliothèque de l'Institut de France

decided to continue the palace complex. The court architect Zuccalli thus also resumed his activities on the site. From 1702/03 the present side pavilions were built from plans by Zuccalli drawn up in 1701–1702, which show Nymphenburg as a complex with five pavilions.

The construction was supervised from 1702 by Antonio Viscardi. The shell of the new side pavilions, which were connected with the main pavilion by galleries, was completed with incredible speed in 1702–1703, probably due to the fact that the builders made use of the old foundations of the pavilions and galleries.

It was then that the concept was developed on which all further additions were based, that of a staggered arrangement of buildings with openings into the park, which fundamentally distinguishes Nymphenburg from compact palaces such as Versailles. The front of the palace, on the town side, is linked with the park not only by openings in the gallery buildings, but also by the passage through the ground floor of the central building, constructed at the time so that vehicles could be driven through it.

With the pairs of pavilions forward of the main building, Nymphenburg was enlarged to create a wide cour d'hon-

neur on the town side. It is thus similar to the Dutch palace Het Loo (1685–1687) with its staggered cube-shaped pavilions. Since Max Emanuel was at the time allied with the palace's patron, William III of Orange, this idea might have been borrowed from Het Loo, especially since the ideas of the country's leading architect Daniel Marot had found particular favour with the elector.

Allegory of Elector Max Emanuel's return from exile (detail), François Roettier, 1715, main palace (Room 12)

With the expansion of the palace complex, changes were also made to the main pavilion. On both the town and the park side, Zuccalli inserted two rows of huge round-arched windows, one above the other, which made the original solid-looking building with its small windows unusually transparent.

The façade of the central building at this time was divided up by lisenes, cut through by a moulding above the upper row of round-arched windows. Today this pattern is still reflected on the town side of the palace, where the massive pilasters only reach as far as this string course.

At the same time as the exterior was being altered, the interior of the Great Hall also underwent a major transformation. The west wall was opened on the first and second floor, thus also letting light from this side into the room. The two halls one above the other on the park side were connected with the Great Hall by a double row of arcades. The portals to the apartments on the side walls remained and the large room, which – including the transverse oval windows – was then already the height it is today, was additionally decorated with pilasters and the present console moulding.

Work on the interior of the Great Hall commenced in September 1701. Johann Anton Gumpp was responsible for the painting until 1703. As was appropriate for a hunting lodge and summer residence, the ceiling was decorated with scenes from the legend of Diana. And as in Lustheim Palace, which was also decorated by Gumpp, the central painting depicted Jupiter granting Diana hunting rights. Four accompanying pictures showed the goddess as a

View of Nymphenburg Palace from the park side, Franz Joachim Beich, 1722/23, main palace, North Gallery (Room 9)

huntress surrounded by her nymphs. The hall walls were covered with nine huge paintings of scenes from the life of the hunting goddess Diana that reached from the moulding to the floor. In 1726 these pictures seem to have been replaced by paintings on leather, the work of the Valeriani brothers in Venice, which were specially ordered for the Great Hall in Nymphenburg by Max Emanuel.

The theme of the paintings in the Great Hall – as well as in the hunting lodge of Lustheim near Schleißheim – which also include rare scenes from the life of Diana, are probably based on the work of the humanist at the Turin court, Emanuele Tesauro. He had already compiled a comprehensive cycle of material from the Diana legend for Venaria Reale, the hunting lodge of Adelaide's parents near Turin.

In the period from 1701 to 1703, the electoral apartments in the main building of Nymphenburg Palace were also altered. According to a report by Henrico Zuccalli, from 19 April 1701 on, artisans and stucco-workers were busy decorating the apartments adjacent to the Great Hall. On 2 November 1701 five paintings for the ceiling were brought into the palace from the palace farm and hung up. These were probably the canvas paintings completed in around 1675 by Triva, Zanchi, Catani and Werner, which had either been stored in the farm after the death of Ferdinand Maria (1679) or kept here while the renovation work was in progress. These paintings of ancient gods can still be seen today in the apartments on either side of the Great Hall. In one place stucco-work from this time has also been preserved, which according to the building accounts may have been by Pietro F. A. Appiani from Porta near Milan.

The extension of Nymphenburg was held up by the outbreak of the War of the Spanish Succession and the defeat at Höchstädt (Battle of Blenheim) in 1704. It was only when Max Emanuel returned from exile after the Rastatt Peace Treaty of 7 March 1714 that building activities could be fully resumed.

Nymphenburg
aussen

SECOND BUILDING PERIOD UNDER MAX EMANUEL

The court architect Joseph Effner, Jacopo Amigoni, 1720/21, Schleißheim New Palace

The further extension of the palace was in the hands of Joseph Effner. Effner, the son of a Dachau gardener, was brought by Max Emanuel to Paris for training in 1706. Only a year later, the elector sent Effner to study architecture in the office of the well-known architect Germain Boffrand. In 1714, while still in Paris, Effner was appointed head of the Nymphenburg project. In 1715 he became an electoral court architect and in 1724 – after the death of Zuccalli – chief architect at court.

In 1714 he began to turn the lisenes of the main pavilion into pilasters, reinforcing them on the garden side and taking them up to the eaves cornice. It was also at this time that the number of windows flanking the large arches in the central building was reduced from four to three, as is first depicted in Franz Joachim Beich's 1723 view of the palace. In 1726 Charles Dubut was paid for the stucco reliefs above the windows. The central building acquired large triangular gables (removed in 1826) above the three central axes. Effner was thus responsible for the final form of the façade.

Joseph Effner developed a new overall concept whereby the farm on the south side was transformed into an extensive building complex, which was to be mirrored by a similar complex to the north. On the south side were the court stables with the apartments of the cavaliers (now the location of the Marstallmuseum and the Museum of Nymphenburg Porcelain). The various sections of the building were completed in 1719, 1733 and 1747. The keystones of the arch over the driveway are marked "CA 1740" and the building is the work of Joseph Effner, Johann Gunezrhainer and François Cuvilliés the Elder. On the north side of the palace the Orangery was built as its counterpart; its corner risalit, the so-called Johannis Tower, had already been erected in 1716. The Orangery itself was not however completed until 1755/57.

ELECTOR MAX EMANUEL OF BAVARIA (1662–1726)

Elector Max Emanuel saw himself in the role of heroic prince. Fame and esteem – as his mother had taught him – were best achieved by means of aggressive policies and generous patronage. Very soon after he took over the government in 1680, the young prince participated in the Turkish war and became the emperor's most important aide. In 1685 he married the emperor's daughter Maria Antonia and in 1691 was promoted to the position of governor of the Spanish Netherlands. He then transferred his court to Brussels and governed abroad for around 20 years. In 1701 the elector became an ally of France in order to achieve the longed-for elevation of rank in the Spanish War of Succession (1701–1714). In 1704 he lost Bavaria in the catastrophic defeat of Höchstädt (Battle of Blenheim) and went into exile in France. He returned to Bavaria in 1715, where he was successful in organizing politically advantageous marriages and influential church positions for his children. Although his record in the political arena is very mixed, it is in the area of art that his achievements exceeded those of all the other Bavarian rulers. It is due to Max Emanuel's collections of paintings that the city of Munich rose to become a European art metropolis.

The long façades with their separately roofed central and corner pavilions, the uniform rows of blind arcades on the ground floor and segmental arched windows on the upper floor identify the buildings as an example of what was then "modern" French architecture, of which Effner had had first-hand experience when he was studying in Paris. The south inner courtyard of Nymphenburg is surprisingly similar to Libéral Bruant's "Cour Royale" in the Hôtel des Invalides. In Paris Effner also became acquainted with the new interior decoration forms of the Régence period. He first introduced this style in 1720 in the North Antechamber of the main Nymphenburg building. With the white wall panelling and gilt carvings, which depicted war trophies and emblems of the arts, he laid the foundation for the interior decoration of the Rococo period which was soon to flourish under François Cuvilliés the Elder.

Elector Max Emanuel (detail), Joseph Vivien, 1706, Munich Residence

One of the most important workshops at the court of Max Emanuel was that of the sculptors, who included Guillielmus de Grof from Antwerp, the Parisian sculptor Charles Dubut and the Italian Giuseppe Volpini. The Paris-trained cabinet-maker, ornamental carver and gilder Johann Adam Pichler headed the workshop responsible for all the wooden carving.

The painters working on Nymphenburg at the time were the popular Italian Jacopo Amigoni, the Tirolean Johann Anton Gumpp and succeeding him Nikolaus Gottfried Stuber, also Franz Joachim Beich from Ravensburg and the French artists Joseph Vivien, Nicolas Bertin and François Roettier.

Near the end of Max Emanuel's life, in 1723 and 1724, two-storey buildings connecting the main palace with the stables and Orangery were completed, the Comedy and Orangery House on the south side (later turned into the kitchen block) and a building for a ball game ("Pass-Spiel") and billiards on the north side. The connecting galleries across the canals were built at a later date: the so-called

Marstall court-yard, façade of the east tract

north water corridor in 1739, and its equivalent on the south side only after Gunezrhainer took over the building operations in 1745. Effner was also the architect of the three garden buildings created for Max Emanuel: in the northern half of the park the Pagodenburg with an interior in the newly fashionable chinoiserie style (1716–1719), and in the southern half the Badenburg (1719–1721), a rare example of an early 18th century bathing palace. In the final year of Max Emanuel's life, Effner embarked on a hermitage, the Magdalenenklause: the ageing elector wanted a place of retreat for devotional meditation, but did not, however, live to see it completed.

NYMPHENBURG UNDER KARL ALBRECHT, 1726–1745

Under Elector Karl Albrecht (from 1742 Karl VII, Emperor of the Holy Roman Empire of the German Nation) a "Carlstadt" was planned, which was almost certainly also the work of Effner. It was probably modelled on Karlsruhe, which has a similar lay-out: the palace stands in the middle of a crescent, with the streets of the town – never completed in Nymphenburg – radiating out from it. The first crescent building was constructed in 1728 on the south side (for court inspector Hieber) and the last building, which from 1761 housed the porcelain manufactory, in 1758 on the north side. Even before the "Carlstadt" project there were plans to turn the extensive cour d'honneur on the town side into a park with canals, pools, green areas and a fountain. The idea of designing a cour d'honneur as a garden, originating from Joseph Effner, son of a gardener, and Dominique Girard, was completely novel. The next step was to surround the garden with the crescent which, with its two-storey buildings linked by low walls, also connected the ends of the extensive palace complex. The impression which the Nymphenburg cour d'honneur made on the people of the time was described in 1784 by the St Gallen monastery librarian P. Johannes Nepomuk Hauntinger as follows: "Here you see an extraordinarily magnificent array of buildings; together they form an absolutely uniform amphitheatre which is exceptionally beautiful. At the centre of this amphitheatre, dominating all the other buildings, is the splendid palace, which is entered via two grand flights of marble steps embellished with balustrades, vases and lions. Extending from both sides of this central point is a semicircle of buildings, which can all be seen at once and which are perfectly symmetrical".

The planned "Carlstadt", however, involved not just extending the palace complex with the crescent, but also creating

Next double page: Nymphenburg palace and garden complex, Johann Adam von Zisla, c. 1723, Munich, State Graphics Collection

CHATEAU DE NIMPHENBOURG
Explication.
Le grand Pauillion.
Salleriez des Tablaux.
Pauillion de S. A. E.
Pauillion des Princes.
La Chapelle.
Logement des Gentilshommes.
Aßamblée des Jeus.
Le Theatre.
Passages de Communications.
Les offices.
Les Escuries et Remises.
Les Hostelleries.
La Baße Cour.
Le Mannege.
La Mesnagerie.
Le Potager.
Petits Jardins des
Bosquets.
Theatre d'Eaux.
deux Parterres.
Le grand Bassin.

A. E. DE BAVIERE
e Paße.
, d'Eaux.
Maille auec une piesse,
des Pagottes.
Eaux.
27 Estoilles de gazon.
28 Le Canal. 29. La Cascade de Marbre
30 Parterre d'Eaux.
31 Pauillion des Beignes.
32 La Machine Pour les Eaux.
33 grande Cour, en face du grand Pau
34 deux Petites Cours de Cottez.
35 La Cascade deuant le Chataux.
36 avenues.
37 Piping village.
38 Paßing village.
39 Menzing Chataux de M.me l'Electric
40 Unter Menzing village.
41 Ola village.
J. A. Zisla Ing: Fecit.

a settlement along the two drives on either side of the palace canal. This was intended for artisans and tradesmen, whose trade, legal rights and several years of tax exemption would be protected by the court. In return, however, they were expected to build their houses and lay out their gardens at their own expense in accordance with specific guidelines. The new settlement was also to include artists: one of the most important representatives of this group to move into a house in Carlstadt was the court cabinet-maker and ornamental carver Johann Adam Pichler, who frequently worked in the Munich Residence and Nymphenburg. However, new residents had already ceased to arrive by the 1740s and a few decades later this town-planning project had been forgotten.

Elector Karl Albrecht as Emperor Karl VII (detail), atelier of George Desmarées, after 1742, main palace (Room 10)

The extensive stables grouped around the large courtyard in the rectangular building on the south side of the palace were also a remarkable construction. After the idea of the massive west tract was given up, probably at the latest with the death of Max Emanuel (the present administrative tract housing the Bavarian Palace Department dates from 1986/89), there were various projects with a generally more open west side where the park formed a backdrop to the courtyard. This is how, for example, it is shown in a drawing by the "court engineer" Johann Adam von Zisla (p. 26/27): the first courtyard ended in an arena which was separated from the garden by a curved wrought-iron fence. At the transition to the park there was to have been a flat-roofed building with five axes which, according to the legend on Zisla's drawing, was intended as a menagerie. What is certain is that the counterpart to the west wing that is shown on this spot in 18th-century veduttas was never actually built.

Karl Albrecht's favourite architect (from 1725 on) was François Cuvilliés the Elder, a Walloon and former court dwarf at Max Emanuel's court, who had received his architectural training in Paris. For the Nymphenburg palace

ELECTOR KARL ALBRECHT (1697–1745)

When Karl Albrecht took over the government in 1726, he was equipped like few of his predecessors to maintain the important political position of the Electorate of Bavaria. Karl Albrecht was born in 1697 in Brussels. While his father was in exile he was a prisoner of the Austrians. But after the family was reunited in 1715, Max Emanuel ensured that the prince received a proper education and gave him personal instruction in politics. Karl Albrecht also pursued the same basic political aim as his father: as the male line of the Habsburgs was about to die out, the imperial title should once again be conferred on a member of the House of Wittelsbach after being so long in the hands of the Austrians. During his first years of government the elector successfully pursued an austerity policy, but from 1730 large sums were invested in the military, and in particular in building projects and promotion of the arts. His aim was to demonstrate his claim to the imperial title with a magnificent court, and by copying the artistic style of the French court he was also making a political statement: he was attempting to outshine Vienna. However, Karl Albrecht, crowned emperor with great pomp and ceremony in Frankfurt am Main in 1742, was unable to enforce his dynastic claims with military action. After his early death in 1745, Bavaria sank back into political obscurity.

complex he designed the little hunting lodge Amalienburg, considered to be the most perfect example of German Rococo art. Foremost among the artisans responsible for the interior were the brilliant stucco-worker Johann Baptist Zimmermann and the Munich cabinet-maker and ornamental carver Joachim Dietrich. However, the deviser of the extraordinarily beautiful decoration was without a doubt François Cuvilliés, one of the greatest designers of the century, who excelled in the creation of the most intricate Rococo ornamentation.

Elector Max III Joseph and Count von Salern in the North Cabinet (woodturning cabinet), Johann Jakob Dorner, 1765, main palace (Room 4)

MAX III JOSEPH AND NYMPHENBURG, 1745–1777

Elector Max III Joseph, the last elector of the Rococo age, completed numerous unfinished projects in Nymphenburg, as well as in the Munich Residence and in Schleißheim. All the remaining building work was accomplished, for example in the crescent and in particular the north wing with the Orangery tract, which was only completed by Johann Gunezrhainer in 1755/57. On its upper floor, in addition to guest apartments (no longer in existence), was the Hubertus Hall with nine window axes, which supplemented the Great Hall as a venue for festivities and theatrical performances. Under Max III Joseph, all four park buildings were renovated and the park was decorated with the marble statues of which there had previously been only rather random examples, often of a provisory nature. Shortly before his death, the conversion of the Green Hall in the connecting tract on the south side into a dining hall for the cavaliers was begun; at the same time the kitchen was moved from the neighbouring building to the ground floor of the same tract.

Max III Joseph also renovated and redecorated many of the rooms in Nymphenburg Palace. The most important room, the Great Hall, acquired a colourful new interior by

ELECTOR MAX III JOSEPH (1727–1777)

"If no-one else wants peace, I do!" said the eighteen-year-old elector Max III Joseph, and in 1745 put an end to an era of power politics with the Peace of Füssen. Further war-making would probably also have been pointless with the Austrian army marching on Bavaria and forty million guilders of debt inherited from his father. After concluding peace with the Habsburgs, Max Joseph pursued a policy of neutrality. This gave him the opportunity to start reforming the country. Life at the Munich court was on a much more frugal scale than before. But in spite of the empty coffers, after a failed harvest, the elector bought cheap grain in Italy and distributed it to the population. Max III Joseph introduced the potato to Bavaria, founded the Bavarian Academy of Sciences and from 1771 made school compulsory. There was much less money for building projects. However, he did commission the Cuvilliés Theatre, probably the most beautiful Rococo theatre in the world, and the Great Hall of Nymphenburg. When the reformer died in 1777 with no heirs, it was with a popular ruler that the old Bavarian line of the House of Wittelsbach came to an end.

Johann Baptist Zimmermann appropriate to its function as a festival and concert hall. François Cuvilliés the Elder, who had returned in 1755 from his second stay in Paris, seems to have been less involved in Zimmermann's design than was previously assumed; however, the white wall decoration in the Garden Hall and Gallery Hall (Music Gallery) is without a doubt his work. In its final version, the huge ceiling fresco in the main hall once again depicted the goddess Flora and the nymphs, to whom Electress Adelaide had dedicated her summer residence ninety years previously. Cuvilliés was also clearly involved in the alteration of the two corner cabinets in the palace in 1763/64. The rocaille ornamentation of the ceilings is the work of Franz Xaver Feichtmayr the Younger, who became the court stucco-worker in Munich after the death of Johann Baptist Zimmermann.

A number of other artisans were employed in the redecoration of the palace in the 1750s and 60s. The Nymphenburg porcelain painter Johann Härringer painted wall panels with chinoiseries, while ornamental carving and sculpture were still being supplied by the large workshop of Johann Adam Pichler, where his son and successor Joseph Adam Pichler also began working. Also involved were the ornamental carvers Simon Pruckher and Tobias Grün, the ornamental carver Johann Caspar Hörspurcher and the sculptor Johann Thomas Sailler, who both specialized in carved furniture, the cabinet-maker Johann Georg Eggerer (simpler furniture), the ebenist Georg Sebastian Guglhör, the renowned court gilder Lorenzo Bigarello and the gilders Johann Murpöck and Johann Georg Frauenholz, the embroiderer Fr. J. A. Jansen, the metal-workers Johann Joseph Kraus and Joseph Stürzer (fire irons and metal fittings) and the grotto specialist Anton Langenburcher (glass chandeliers).

Elector Max III Joseph (detail), George Desmarées, 1755, Munich Residence

Next double page: Nymphenburg Palace from the town side, Bernardo Bellotto, known as Canaletto, 1761, Munich Residence

ELECTOR KARL THEODOR, 1777–1799

Under Karl Theodor, the first elector from the Palatinate line, the gallery tracts between the main building and the first side pavilions were widened (1795). Although this resulted in three very liveable rooms in each tract facing the park, the garden could no longer be seen from the gallery rooms. The façades were also completely renovated. Most importantly, Karl Theodor was responsible for summoning the Palatinate court gardener Friedrich Ludwig Sckell to Munich. By 1792, the elector had already opened Nymphenburg Park to the public.

Elector Max IV Joseph, subsequently King Max I Joseph, probably by Simon Petrus Klotz, before 1806, Munich Residence

CHANGES UNDER MAX IV JOSEPH, 1799–1826, FROM 1806 KING MAX I

When Bavaria became a kingdom, King Max I, whose favourite residence was Nymphenburg and who also died here, had large sections of the palace rebuilt. The building project was begun in 1806 under the direction of Karl Ludwig Puille, son of the court architect Charles Pierre Puille who died in 1805, and of Andreas Gärtner. The building records of 1806–1808 list work on the "New Rooms" of the king on the ground floor of the first pavilion on the south side and on the "New Apartments" of the queen on the floor above. The first pavilion on the north side was also altered, with the loss of most of the 18th-century interiors as a result.

In keeping with the fashions of the time, the rooms were austere and simple, but the furnishings exquisitely beautiful. The Study (Room 16), the Audience Chamber (Room 19) and the Queen's Bedroom (Room 20) are still uniformly decorated with silk wall coverings, sopraportas and fine furniture.

Even before the renovation of the palace, the nature-loving Max Joseph had commissioned Friedrich Ludwig Sckell

KING MAX I JOSEPH (1756–1825)

When the unpopular elector Karl Theodor 1799 died, Max IV Joseph from the Zweibrücken-Birkenfeld line took over the government of Bavaria. The new ruler was faced with massive problems. Bavaria was caught between revolutionary France and conservative Austria, which was threatening to annex it. However, with the signing of the Bavarian-French treaty in 1801, the country embarked on a period of fruitful partnership with France under Napoleon. The elevation of Bavaria to a kingdom, which was Napoleon's reward to his ally after the victory at Austerlitz (2.12.1805), was a deliberate political move on the part of the French emperor. In 1806 Bavaria thus achieved full political sovereignty, territorial expansion and unity. The way was now clear for the implementation of a thorough reform programme, which was drawn up by King Max I Joseph and his minister Count Montgelas. The crowning achievement of this popular king was the Bavarian constitution of 1818. Important aspects of state reform, liberal civil rights and the separation of state and dynasty were established at this time. Nymphenburg with its gardens became the favourite place of the nature-loving monarch, who was particularly interested in botany.

to turn the grounds into a landscape park of the English type. With the park and the renovated rooms, Nymphenburg was now an important early 19th-century residence. In 1826 Leo von Klenze altered the central building in the Neoclassical style. The gables with the coat of arms of the Bavarian electors and a massive cornice supported by wooden consoles were removed in an attempt to do justice to contemporary tastes in architecture.

THE PARK

An electoral "pleasure garden" was associated with the summer residence of Nymphenburg from the outset. The original grounds laid out for Electress Adelaide were still of modest proportions, but in 1701 Max Emanuel embarked on the development of one of the finest parks in Germany, summoning first Le Nôtre pupil Charles Carbonet (1701), and later Dominique Girard (from 1715) from Paris for the purpose. It was then that the wide canal branching from the River Würm and entering the park by the Large Cascade was created to form the central axis. By 1730 its counterpart on the town side had been completed, together with the two splendid avenues. The Cascade was designed by Effner. In 1731, however, Girard had what is described in the records as the "lamentable upper cascade" reconstructed in conglomerate and "faced the surfaces over which the water flowed with marble". In 1768, under Elector Max III, the court stone mason Joseph Cajetan Linsinger began to face the entire basin in red and grey marble.

The Large Parterre west of the palace was divided into eight sections with flowerbeds in the middle. At the centre was the Flora basin by Guillielmus de Grof, to which dragon and dolphin fountains were added at a later date. The parterre was flanked by boskets or hedge gardens, such as the summer orangery with orange trees in tubs;

Nymphenburg palace and garden complex before the transformation of the Baroque park into an English landscape garden, artist unknown, 1755

there was also a garden for the "Pass-Spiel" ball game and one for a popular Russian version of the game of nine-pins, each with little open pavilions ("cabinets à jour"), and a maze with an open-air theatre enclosed by hedges.
In these geometrically designed gardens the Pagodenburg and the Badenburg with their parterres, fountains and clipped hedges were originally the architectural focal points of the horizontal axis (although this was not actu-

The royal court garden superintendent Friedrich Ludwig von Sckell, Clemens von Zimmermann, c. 1810, Munich Municipal Museum

ally open to view from end to end). The Magdalenenklause was built in the side bosket in the north part of the gardens, a "lonely and melancholy area". The small pavilion-like building on a sketch by Franz Joachim Beich, which is located at the centre of an octagonal star opposite the Magdalenenklause on the spot where the Amalienburg was later built, is almost certainly the work of Effner. The Amalienburg was also originally surrounded by a strictly geometric garden, continuing the pattern of the interior. A curved hedge enclosed the small cour d'honneur on the west side of the hunting lodge. From 1733 a wall was built

round the entire park, with gates at the ends of the main axes to make it possible to look from the gardens, where nature had been "shaped" to the untamed open countryside beyond.
Max Emanuel had already laid out two small gardens with parterres next to the electoral living quarters. In 1757 the charming octagonal Aviary (designed by François Cuvilliés the Elder) was built for Max III Joseph in the garden on the south side. The building was painted inside and out by Ambrosius Hörmannstorffer and fragments of the delightful façade (restored several times) still remain, featuring putti at play, bouquets of flowers in vases, garlands and flying birds. In 1768 François Cuvilliés the Younger built the so-called Small Cascade in the same garden, based on plans by Dominique Girard dating from 1724. Max III Joseph also had the gardens decorated with a large number of marble sculptures and vases.
In the early 19th century (1804–1823), the Baroque bosket gardens with their symmetrical pattern were transformed by the brilliant landscape gardener Friedrich Ludwig von Sckell into the landscape garden of the type that had already been popular in England since the beginning of the 18th century. Von Sckell, who in one of his essays ("Beiträge zur Bildenden Gartenkunst") expresses the opinion that majestic avenues that harmonize with the architecture not only convey an impression of splendour and luxury, but are also of practical use to the people walking in the park, retained the basic features of the Baroque garden. By basing his landscape garden on the Large Parterre and the central canal he thus gave his creation the unique character for which it is greatly admired.
The irregularly shaped palace park is surrounded by a wall that was not completed until 1735. This construction has always been rather fragile and is often in need of repair, as it is just a simple brick wall only half a brick thick even though it is stabilised on the park side with projec-

tions resembling pier buttresses. The top of the wall has been recapped with hollow semicircular tiles, as it was in the beginning; the piers are bevelled and covered like the surfaces of the wall with a thin coating of plaster. At points where the wall changes direction there are several small round towers with conical roofs, where the guards could shelter.

In the 18th century there were gates in the wall at the end of the avenues that crossed the Baroque garden, but these

Pagodenburg with Baroque garden parterre, Franz Joachim Beich, 1722/23, main palace, North Gallery (Room 9)

were closed off when von Sckell converted Nymphenburg into a landscape park. Instead, at four points where there was a view of the countryside beyond the boundary of the park, the park wall was sunk. Because of the exclamations of surprise uttered by those who encountered the hidden walls, they are known as ha-has.

In some of the main axes of the parks are simple iron gates originating from Baroque times, roughly made but adequately serving their purpose.

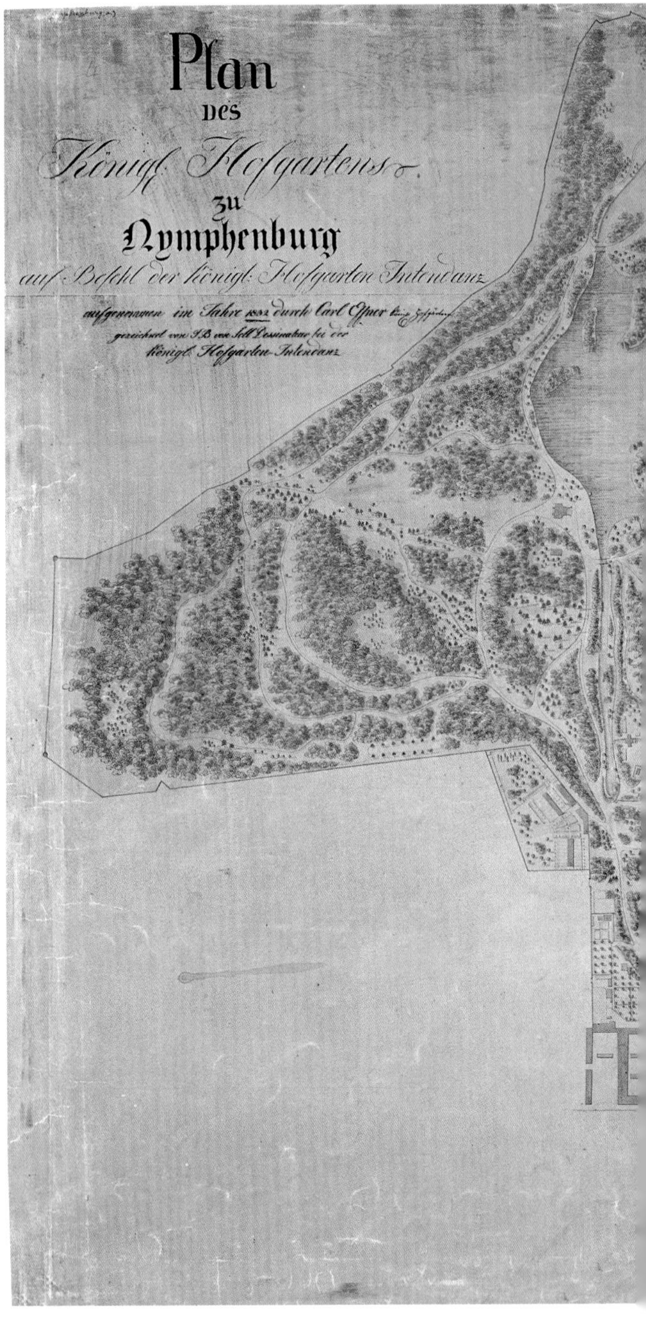
Plan
des
Königl. Hofgartens
zu
Nymphenburg
auf Befehl der königl. Hofgarten Intendanz
gezeichnet von J. B. von Sell Dessinateur bei der
königl. Hofgarten-Intendanz

The landscape garden of Nymphenburg Palace, plan of the completed garden by Carl Effner sr. and Johann Baptist von Sell, 1832

Tour
The main palace

1 GREAT HALL

Main palace, Great Hall (Room 1)

The overwhelming effect of this hall is produced by a combination of large-scale room architecture and lavish decoration. The room architecture, a framework of high pilasters with composite capitals, architrave, frieze and console moulding, was applied in its basic form to the initially plain walls by Henrico Zuccalli in 1702 and decorated in 1756 by Johann Baptist Zimmermann. The round-arched windows on either side are a further dominant feature of the hall, not only filling the huge room with light but also

The main palace, plan of the first floor

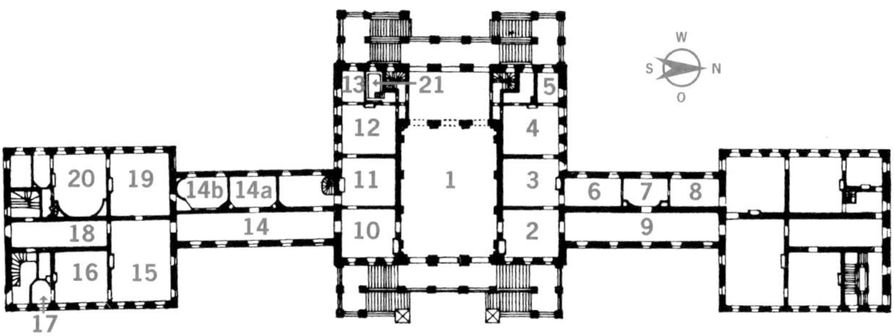

1 Great Hall
2 North Antechamber
3 Antechamber
4 Former Bedroom
5 North Cabinet
6 Max Emanuel's Great Gallery of Beauties
7 Coat of Arms Room
8 Karl Theodor Room
9 North Gallery
10 South Antechamber
11 Antechamber
12 Bedroom
13 Chinese Lacquer Cabinet
14 South Gallery
14 a+b Antechamber and Writing Cabinet of Elector Karl Theodor

Queen's Apartment

15 Former Dining Room/King Ludwig I's Gallery of Beauties
16 Study (Burl Room)
17 Cabinet
18 Small Gallery
19 Audience Chamber (Blue Salon)
20 Bedroom
21 Bathroom

Ceiling fresco, Great Hall, (Room 1)

opening it both on the town side, and, across the two interposed halls at the back, on the park side. A seamless transition to both outside areas is provided with external flights of steps, which were characteristic of Nymphenburg from the beginning. Since there was then no need for a grand staircase inside, it was possible to build a Great Hall of unusually large dimensions. This in particular identifies Nymphenburg as a summer palace.

In 1755–1757, Max III Joseph had the Great Hall and the two adjacent halls on the garden side redesigned with the participation of François Cuvilliés the Elder. The lavish Rococo stucco-work on the walls and vault with numerous musical motifs was produced by the elderly Johann Baptist Zimmermann in 1755/56. In the corners large figures representing the four seasons with groups of putti between them bearing the symbols of the 12 months. A border of green- and red-tinted grisaille painting frames the large ceiling fresco, which is also the work of Johann Baptist Zimmermann. The master was assisted by his son Franz Michael, and in particular by his pupil Martin Heigl, who in 1757 received court protection as a reward for his work on the wall and ceiling frescos of the hall.

In order to emphasize the character of the palace, the "park landscape" is continued in the frescos. The basic theme of the ceiling fresco, according to a description in the painting inventory of 1758 written shortly after its completion, was the role of Nymphenburg as the summer residence of the electoral family: the "esteemed electoral gods and nymphs of Bavaria", represented by Olympian gods, are in the process of establishing themselves in the pleasure garden of the goddess Flora. The idyllic scenes celebrate the flourishing of the Wittelsbach dynasty (and the Bavarian state under their rule) and the promotion of the fine arts under Max III Joseph as a prince of peace. The colour scheme of the hall is particularly attractive with white and gold for the architectural framework and a delicate green

Abduction of Flora by the west wind Zephyr, ceiling fresco, Garden Hall bordering the Great Hall (Room 1)

for the wall panels that serve as a background to the colourful wall paintings. This forms a transition to the colour symphony of the ceiling fresco. The gilding was under the direction of Lorenzo Bigarello, who had already been active at the court for several decades.

On the park side of the ceiling fresco spanning the entire room, nymphs pay homage to the nymph Flora who has become a goddess, a reference to the name of the palace. The other scenes around the edge of the vault deal with beauty care (Badenburg!), hunting, music and festivals as forms of entertainment in the park: on the left Venus at her toilet on a bed of clouds, on the right, Diana, goddess of hunting; on the town side, in a park setting, Minerva and Orpheus instruct the muses of music and the arts, while the drunken Bacchus sleeps beneath a canopy. (Orpheus is probably a reference to the Bavarian elector's love of music.) In the centre of the ceiling, Apollo rides on the sun chariot surrounded by Olympian gods; Mercury proclaims the fame of the house with his trumpet and next to him is Zephyr, whose breath causes Flora's garden to bloom. Mars, the bringer of war, is excluded from this peaceful gathering and relegated to the bottom left-hand corner of the picture.

The picture in the middle of the left-hand wall shows Cephalus and Procris and the picture on the right-hand wall Mars and Venus, while above the doors are pastoral scenes as allegories of the four humours. The comprehensive picture programme is continued in the stucco figures above the cornice.

François Cuvilliés the Elder was probably commissioned to design the inner door pediments and the stucco décor of the white annex rooms on the main and gallery floors towards the end of 1756. The work was again carried out by Zimmermann's workshop. Zimmermann's ceiling pictures in these two rooms are in small sections by contrast with the expansive design of the large main fresco.

The ceiling of the Garden Hall shows the abduction of Flora by Zephyr. The stucco trophies on the pillars refer to ancient gods. On the ceiling of the music gallery is a representation of Latona transforming the Lycian peasants into frogs (from Ovid's Metamorphoses). One section of the wall is beautifully decorated with realistically sculpted reliefs of numerous musical instruments. Elector Max III Joseph was a great music-lover, and was himself a good gamba player and composer.

The Great Hall has remained unchanged since 1758. With the exception of dusting and small improvements within reach of the users, it has not been touched, so that it has been preserved as an authentic Rococo room. The restoration work in 1990/95 was again limited to cleaning and to filling and retouching the cracks and gaps that had since appeared.

Carved weapons trophy, Johann Adam Pichler, 1716/17, North Antechamber (Room 2)

Furnishings: The six Neoclassical crystal chandeliers made in around 1810 with twelve matching sconces have been hung up again; they were first installed in place of the seven original Rococo chandeliers when Bavaria became a kingdom. ■ The pair of console tables designed in around 1723/24 by Effner were only installed in Nymphenburg Palace in 1885. These elaborate tables produced in the Pichler workshop were among the original items of furniture in the Victory Hall in the Schleißheim New Palace, which was completed in 1725.

NORTH WING

The apartment in the central building (Rooms 2–5) which in the first decoration phase (under Henriette Adelaide) was intended for the elector, was used as an elegant guest apartment after the extension of the palace under Max Emanuel. The elector lived in the first north pavilion, which was decorated from 1716, and consisted of a state apartment on the main floor, a private apartment on the 2nd floor and the assembly rooms on the ground floor. Today the rooms in the first north pavilion (known since the 19th century as the Crown Prince Building), which are accessed through the north gallery, are not open to the public.

2 NORTH ANTECHAMBER

The North Antechamber and the adjacent gallery formed the entrance to Max Emanuel's state apartment in the north pavilion and marked the beginning of a magnificent suite of

Main palace, North Antechamber (Room 2)

rooms. The gold-and-white wooden panelling in the French Régence style was designed by the court architect Effner and carved in around 1720 by the court cabinet-maker and ornamental carver Johann Adam Pichler, who also trained in Paris. The wall decoration celebrates the elector's military fame. The portrait on the back wall thus shows Max Emanuel as the victor of Namur – one of his few successes in the Spanish War of Succession (Joseph Vivien, 1711). The panelled ceiling was completed in around 1675 during the first building period of the palace: in the central oval is

The goddess Ceres, ceiling painting by Antonio Zanchi, c. 1675, North Antechamber (Room 2)

Ceres in a chariot pulled by dragons, painted by Antonio Zanchi; in the corner panels are putti bearing the gifts of Ceres, painted by Johann Anton Gumpp.

Other paintings: The sopraportas with children at play as allegories of the four elements were painted by Jacopo Amigoni in 1716. ■ Opposite the fireplace is a portrait of the second wife of Max Emanuel, Therese Kunigunde of Poland, by Franz Joseph Winter after an original by Vivien.

Furniture: The console table made c. 1720 from a design by Effner was part of the furnishing of the Great Hall together with three other identical tables. After the hall was redecorated (1755–1757), two of the console tables were installed in the antechambers.

Clock: The mantelpiece clock with its rich veneer of reddish tortoiseshell and gilt metal inlays comes from what was once a large collection of furniture in the "classical" Boulle technique, which Max Emanuel brought to Bavaria from the Spanish Netherlands and France. The clock is from the Residence Palace and in the 19th century was in the Outer Audience Chamber of the Rich Rooms. The creator of the case – the ebenist Henry van Soest from Antwerp – has most unusually signed his work on the small plaque underneath the clock face. Van Soest's boldness in this respect is associated with his special position as a wholesaler who not only supplied Max Emanuel with luxury furniture and expensive wine but also functioned for a time as his treasurer during his years of exile. The clockwork is by the Parisian clockmaker Gosselin. The clock is dated between 1700 and 1710.

Mantlepiece clock, Henry van Soest, Paris, 1700–1710, North Antechamber (Room 2)

3 ANTECHAMBER

The Baroque panelled ceiling includes a painting by Johann Anton Gumpp: "Mars with Consilium and Inventio above a view of Troy", 1682. The painting is not one of the original pictures from the Adelaide period. It was only installed here later on and comes from the Knights' Hall of the Residence Palace. It is the only remaining ceiling painting from the Alexander Rooms, which Max Emanuel commissioned after taking over the government in 1680, but which were subsequently replaced with rooms of a different layout.

Tapestries: The tapestries were probably acquisitions of Max Emanuel, but were only hung up here in the 20th century. *On the rear wall*: Diana from a series entitled "The Triumphs of the Gods", Brussels, c. 1720, by the combined manufactories of Heinrich Reydams, Urban und Daniel Leyniers, from designs by Jan van Orley and Augustin Coppens. *On the side walls:* March–April and July–August from a series of garden scenes illustrating the months, Brussels, c. 1690, manufactory of Jan Frans van den Hecke.

Family portrait of the Bavarian and Saxon electoral families (detail), Peter Jakob Horemans, 1761, Former Bedroom (Room 4)

Furnishings: Above the fireplace a portrait of Electress Therese Kunigunde in her youth, depicted as Venus with Cupid; painted by Martin Maingaud, Brussels, c. 1699 ■ The writing table (bureau plat) with bronze fittings (Paris, c. 1760) and probably also the rest of the furniture with the console tables (signed by Adam Weisweiler, Paris, c. 1785) and the dainty couch and armchairs (signed Georges Jacob, Paris, c. 1780) belonged to the Palatinate-Zweibrücken line of the Wittelsbach family.

4 FORMER BEDROOM

The central picture of the Baroque panelled ceiling shows the sea goddess Thetis, enthroned on a shell in the clouds, by the Swiss artist Joseph Werner, c. 1674. It is identical with a painting by Werner mentioned in Sandrart's "Teutsche Academie", featuring a "... portrait of Thetis, in the heavens and surrounded by many charming gods, throwing every kind of rare seashell from her chariot, created to the complete satisfaction of your Electoral Highness". The wall panelling was repainted in the 19th century. The blue damask covering on the rear wall was replaced in 1966.

Paintings:
Rear wall, right: Elector Max III Joseph at the lathe with Count von Salern, Johann Jakob Dorner, 1765.

On the rear wall in a carved gilt Rococo frame: Conversation Piece. The Bavarian and Saxon electoral families making music and playing cards: 32 small figures, Peter Jakob Horemans, 1761. Prince Friedrich Christian of Saxony, together with his family and court, lived between 1760 and 1762 during the Prussian occupation of Saxony with his brother-in-law Elector Max III Joseph of Bavaria. The painting records a concert and a game of cards, organized to entertain the court in Nymphenburg Palace. According to the inventory of 1763, the picture hung at that time in the elector's apartments.
On the left-hand wall: Max Emanuel's Little Gallery of Beauties from the elector's bedroom on the upper floor of the Badenburg, which was destroyed in 1944.

Furniture: The French slant-front desk (bureau en pente) with "butterfly wing" motif in rosewood veneer (Paris, c. 1745/50, attributed to Jacques Dubois) was part of a collection of furniture belonging to the Palatinate-Zweibrücken line of the Wittelsbachs which is known to have been used in the north apartment of the main pavilion of Nymphenburg Palace from the beginning of the 19th century. At the time, Duchess Maria Amalia von Zweibrücken (1751–1831), the widowed sister-in-law of King Max Joseph, was using this guest apartment. ■ The little travelling and bed desk, which according to the inscription once belonged to the electoral court theatre director Count Seeau, is an example of the high quality of the south German veneered furniture in the Rococo period (Munich, c.1750). It was probably made by the electoral ebenist Georg Sebastian Guglhör.

Slant-front desk, attributed to Jacques Dubois, Paris, c. 1745/50, Former Bedroom (Room 4)

5 NORTH CABINET

The northern corner cabinet was reduced to its present size under the supervision of François Cuvilliés the Elder in 1763/64 and decorated with

Main palace, North Cabinet (Room 5)

new ceiling stucco-work by Franz Xaver Feichtmayr the Younger. In the corners rocaille cartouches with putti as allegories of the four seasons. The naturalistic stucco-work was restored in its original form in 1950/51.

Furnishings: The walls are decorated with five heads of ancient gods in profile: Bacchus, Mercury, a river god, Ceres and Diana. ■ The rolltop desk from southern Germany (c. 1775–1780) has a magnificent design of musical instruments in marquetry. ■ The twelve-light chandelier is decorated with precious rock crystal drops (c.1765).

6 MAX EMANUEL'S GREAT GALLERY OF BEAUTIES

The three rooms on the garden side of the North Gallery were created when the gallery tract was enlarged under Elector Karl Theodor in 1795. They were refurnished in 1967.

Duchesse de Berry, Pierre Gobert, c. 1715, Max Emanuel's Great Gallery of Beauties (Room 6)

Paintings: Max Emanuel's Great Gallery of Beauties, five portraits of ladies at the court of Louis XIV, which were painted by Pierre Gobert in around 1715 at the same time as the portraits in the Little Gallery of Beauties (Room 4). *From left to right:* Princesse de Conti (daughter of Louis XIV and the Marquise de Montespan) with Cupid, Mademoiselle de Charolois, Duchesse de Berry, Mademoiselle de Clermont, Marquise de Gondrin with Cupid ■ View of the Magdalenenklause, Franz Joachim Beich, c. 1725/30.

7 COAT OF ARMS ROOM

Furnishings: The marble busts portray Elector Karl Theodor as Hercules and his first wife, Elisabeth Auguste von Pfalz-Sulzbach, as Minerva (c. 1780). ■ Four tapestries with the combined coat of arms of the Kurpfalz (Electorate of the Palatinate) and Pfalz-Sulzbach of Elector Karl Theodor and his first wife Elisabeth Auguste, Stephan Boßmann, Savonnerie manufactory Heidelberg-Mannheim, from 1756.

8 KARL THEODOR ROOM

Paintings: Portraits of the Elector Karl Theodor as Grand Master of the Order of St George and his first wife Elisabeth Auguste von Pfalz-Sulzbach, signed and dated on the bottom left: Anton Hickel. f: 1780; the frames are attributed to the sculptor Augustin Egell. ■ *On the window wall* a portrait of the second wife of Elector Karl Theodor, Maria Leopoldine of Austria-Este, signed: Joseph Hauber 1797.

9 NORTH GALLERY

The North Gallery was used for ceremonial entry into Max Emanuel's apartment in the (now inaccessible) north pavilion.

While in the North Antechamber the elector presented himself in his role as a military commander, the North Gallery was designed to glorify him as a builder of palaces, which were of equal importance for the state. In the gallery, the visitors who used to wait here for an audience could study Max Emanuel's numerous building projects in Nymphenburg and elsewhere which were depicted on the large paintings. These informative veduttas, painted by Franz Joachim Beich in 1722/23, give an idea of what the various palace and garden complexes originally looked like.

Marquise de Gondrin with Cupid, Pierre Gobert, c. 1715, Max Emanuel's Great Gallery of Beauties (Room 6)

The pictures are as follows:

On the first window pillar on the right: Nymphenburg Palace from the garden side.

Opposite: Front view of Nymphenburg with the French gardens and the park pavilions in the background. The Amalienburg and the Magdalenenklause were added in by Joseph Stephan in 1760.

On the second window pillar: The hunting lodge of Fürstenried. In the foreground a hunting party, including a small portrait of Elector Max Emanuel.

Opposite: The Badenburg. The little bathing palace is portrayed in the middle of the original French-style Baroque garden with basin, clipped hedges and boskets, which is no longer in existence.

On the third window pillar: Starnberg Palace and the electoral flotilla, dominated by the "Bucentoro", the state galley of Ferdinand Maria and his wife Adelaide, which was modelled by its Italian builder Santurini in the 17th century on the state galley of the Doge of Venice.

Opposite: The once famous Flora basin in the Large Parterre with the Flora group in gilt lead by Guillielmus de Grof (1719) – destroyed in the early 19th century.

On the fourth window pillar: Berg Palace on Lake Starnberg. Favourite residence of Elector Ferdinand Maria. In the foreground a stag hunt in the lake. King Ludwig II, who was born in Nymphenburg Palace (R. 20), drowned near Berg Palace on 13 June 1886.

Main palace, North Gallery (Room 9)

Opposite: The Cascade in Nymphenburg Park, which is still in existence today; the surrounding architecture was never built.
Over the north door: The Pagodenburg with the quatrefoil fountain pool of the original French garden.
Over the south door: The Badenburg.

SOUTH WING

10 SOUTH ANTECHAMBER

Main palace, Antechamber (Room 11)

The Antechamber provided access to the apartments of the electress. Under Elector Max III Joseph the red wall covering was replaced with the present gold-and-white panelling. On the Baroque ceiling from the first building period are paintings by Antonio Domenico Triva, with the water nymph Arethusa in the centre.

Paintings: Sopraportas: Landscapes by Dominicus Nollet, c. 1720 ■ On the walls portraits of Karl Albrecht as Emperor Karl VII and his consort Maria Amalia as empress; atelier of George Desmarées.

11 ANTECHAMBER

On the Baroque panelled ceiling are paintings by Antonio Triva, c. 1675, with the earth goddess Cybele in the centre. Over the marble fireplace is a carved mirror frame, c. 1760/70. The red damask wall covering was recreated in its original form when the room was restored in 1966.

Paintings:
On the rear wall: A double portrait of the palace's founders, Elector Ferdinand Maria and Henriette Adelaide of Savoy, Sebastiano Bombelli, 1666.
On the side walls: Allegorical portraits of the palace's founders, signed by Stefano Catani, dated c. 1675. These paintings, which are some of the oldest interior decorations in Nymphenburg, were installed at a later date in the corner cabinets as oval ceiling paintings, but taken down again when the rooms were redesigned in 1763: Elector Ferdinand Maria as the astronomer Endymion, who by exploring the moon wins the love of Diana (formerly in the south corner cabinet); Electress Henriette Adelaide as Luna-

Diana with her children, Maria Anna as Juno, Clemens Kajetan as Apollo und Violante Beatrix as Flora; on the right Max Emanuel, who, as the future great commander, is being presented with a sword.

Furniture: The room contains original Nymphenburg furniture. The magnificent Florentine table with a top in pietra dura work – birds and twining plants in multicoloured semiprecious stones inlaid in black marble, beginning of the 18th century – is the oldest and most exquisite item of Nymphenburg furniture. It was presented by Grand Duke Cosimo III of Tuscany to the electoral prince Karl Albrecht when he visited Florence in 1716. From 1719 this elaborate piece of furniture served as a desk in Max Emanuel's famous Grand Cabinet (the Depeschenkabinett) in the north pavilion. ■ The pair of chests with gilt bronze fittings were commissioned by Elector Karl Albrecht via the mirror dealer Granier for Nymphenburg Palace. They are two of the finest works produced by the ebenist Bernard II Vanrisamburgh (Paris, c. 1731–1733). Because of their importance they were originally in the electress's bedroom on the main floor of the south pavilion. ■ The two middle armchairs in the group of four beneath the double portrait are from the bedroom of Max III Joseph on the ground floor of the first south pavilion (Munich court workshops, 1767).

Pietra dura table top, Grand Ducal Workshop, Florence, beginning of the 18th century, Antechamber (Room 11)

Chest, Bernard II Vanrisamburgh, Paris, c. 1731–1733, Antechamber (Room 11)

12 BEDROOM

Main palace, Bedroom (Room 12)

On the Baroque panelled ceiling are paintings by Antonio Domenico Triva, c. 1675, with the goddess Flora in the centre. The carved ornamental panel above the fireplace is in the Régence style, c. 1720; the mirror frame on the window wall is from the Rococo period and dates from c. 1760/70. The green damask wall covering was recreated in its original form when the room was restored in 1963.

Max Emanuel and his sister Maria Anna as children, Sebastiano Bombelli, 1666, Bedroom (Room 12)

Paintings:
Above the fireplace: An allegorical representation of the return of the Elector Max Emanuel from exile, 1715, by François Roettier.
On the entrance wall: A portrait of Max Emanuel and his sister Maria Anna as children, Sebastiano Bombelli, 1666.
On the rear wall: Portraits of Elector Max Emanuel and his second wife Therese Kunigunde, signed Johann Andreas Wolff, 1704.

Furnishings: Bed baldachin with silver embroidery on green velvet, Paris, around 1730 ■ The secretary richly decorated with inlaid work showing rustic scenes from Holland and flowers, signed by Jean-Baptiste Saunier and Christophe Wolff, Paris, c. 1760, was probably originally in the Paris palace of Duke Christian IV von Pfalz-Zweibrücken (reigned 1735–1775).

13 CHINESE LACQUER CABINET

The two cabinets in the central pavilion of Nymphenburg were redesigned in 1763/64 under the direction of François Cuvilliés the Elder. He had both rooms made smaller and the ceilings decorated with stucco-work by Franz Xaver Feichtmayr; the room on the south side was turned into a lacquer cabinet featuring a Chinese screen made of Coromandel lacquer, probably purchased by Elector Max Emanuel, and panels by the porcelain maker Johann Härringer.

Main palace, Chinese Lacquer Cabinet (Room 13)

Furniture: The small lacquer cabinet decorated with Japanese lacquer (signed by Claude-Charles Saunier, Paris, c. 1780) and the three lacquered guéridons in the Chinese style with dragons' heads (Munich, c. 1730) add to the exotic atmosphere of this room. Guéridons – small tables for candlesticks which were easy to move around – were an important lighting accessory in the living quarters of the palace.

14 SOUTH GALLERY

The corridor is leading to the electress's (later queen's) apartment, not completed until around 1760. The panelling is much simpler than that of the North Gallery.

Paintings by Franz Joachim Beich, Nikolaus Gottfried Stuber and Joseph Stephan:
On the first window pillar on the left: The Schleißheim New Palace from the garden side, painted by Franz Joachim Beich, with Effner's Baroque façade. In the background an idealized representation of the Old Palace and home farm.
Opposite: View of the Schleißheim palaces by Nikolaus Gottfried Stuber. In the foreground the Old Palace, built by Elector Maximilian I in the early 17th century (badly damaged in the Second World War, the exterior reconstructed in 1971/72 and

the interior in 1985/88). The New Palace of Max Emanuel is shown here with its late Baroque façade, which was altered by Leo von Klenze in 1819. The planned galleries connecting the Old and New Palaces were never built, nor was the Old Palace remodelled in the Baroque style in which it appears here. In the background the palace gardens with Lustheim (built in 1684–1687).

Idealised view of the Schleißheim Old and New Palaces, Nikolaus Gottfried Stuber, South Gallery (Room 14)

On the second window pillar: Lustheim from the east, painted by Franz Joachim Beich (somewhat idealized).
Opposite: Front view of the little garden palace of Lustheim by Franz Joachim Beich. It is surrounded by a semicircular gallery, which was never fully completed and was taken down again in around 1750. In the background the Lustheim canal and the canal which feeds it from the River Isar.
On the third window pillar: Lichtenberg Palace on the River Lech, which was destroyed in the 19th century, painted by Franz Joachim Beich; it was built for Max Emanuel by Henrico Zuccalli as a hunting lodge in the early 18th century. In the foreground, heron hawking.
Opposite: Landshut, painted by Franz Joachim Beich, with St Martin's Church, one of the most important examples of Bavarian late Gothic architecture. Above the town Trausnitz Castle, the ancestral seat of the Wittelsbachs.
On the fourth window pillar: View of Haag Palace east of Munich, by Joseph Stephan, 1756.
Opposite: Dachau Palace built by Duke Albrecht V with its "hanging" gardens, painted by Franz Joachim Beich. It is shown here with four wings, three of which were pulled down in the early 19th century.
Above the entrance: Isareck Palace, by Joseph Stephan, 1757.
Above the exit: Kling Palace near Wasserburg, by Joseph Stephan, 1757.

14 a+b ANTECHAMBER AND WRITING CABINET OF ELECTOR KARL THEODOR

Main palace, Elector Karl Theodor's Writing Cabinet (Room 14 b)

The final extensions to Nymphenburg Palace were made in 1795 by Karl Theodor of Palatinate-Bavaria, after his marriage to Maria Leopoldine of Austria-Este. The two galleries leading to the side pavilions were each widened on the garden side with three cabinets, based on a design by the court architect Maximilian von Verschaffelt. The middle room in the south group served as an anteroom to the Writing Cabinet (left) and a coffee room (right).
In the glass cases in the Antechamber are two groups of figures made of Frankenthal porcelain. *Left:* The Three Fates. *Right:* The Three Graces. (Allegories of the birth and death of the electoral prince Franz Ludwig Joseph, the son of Karl Theodor and his wife Elisabeth Auguste, both 1761). Left and right of the door are two reproductions of copper engravings after Nicolas de Pigage (1723–1796). They show the mosque and the ruin of the Mercury Temple in Schwetzingen Palace Park.

Furnishings: The Writing Cabinet has elegant panelling, with elaborate decoration somewhat in the style of Chinese furniture. ■ The console table is part of the original furnishing. ■ Full use has been made of the corners of the room for wall cupboards, the stove niche and an opening into the neighbouring living room of the electress. The stove is decorated with an open music book and musical instruments. ■ The bust of Elector Karl Theodor at the age of about 30 is by Peter Anton Verschaffelt, the father of the architect.

SOUTH PAVILION

On the main floor of this building were the apartments of first the electresses, and, after 1806, the queens of Bavaria. From Elector Karl Albrecht onwards, the ruler had his apartment on the ground floor of this pavilion.

15 FORMER DINING ROOM/KING LUDWIG I'S GALLERY OF BEAUTIES

In 1807 alterations were made to this building to create apartments on the first floor for Queen Karoline, the consort of King Max I Joseph. The gold-and-white room with its stucco-work sopraportas was originally used as a small dining room. It was then redesigned by Andreas Gärtner, father of the architect Friedrich von Gärtner. Today the Gallery of Beauties of King Ludwig I (reigned 1825–1848), which was originally intended for the Festsaalbau (Festival Hall Building) of the Munich Residence, is displayed here.

Helene Sedlmayr, Joseph Stieler, 1831, King Ludwig I's Gallery of Beauties (Room 15)

Joseph Stieler was commissioned by the king to paint this famous series of beautiful women, not only ladies at the court as in Max Emanuel's Gallery of Beauties (Room 4), but women from all classes of society. From 1827–1850 he produced 36 portraits, of which one (Luise Baroness von Neubeck) was lost, and in 1861 Friedrich Dürck added two more (Carlotta von Breidbach-Bürresheim and Anna Greiner). The best known are probably the "Schöne Münchnerin" (the Beauty of Munich) Helene Sedlmayr, daughter of a shoemaker, and the "Spanish" dancer Lola Montez, cause of the revolution in 1848, when Ludwig I was forced to abdicate.

North wall, left

1 Friederica Catharina, known as Wilhelmine Sulzer, married name Schneider (born 1820), painted 1838
2 Lady Emily Milbanke, née Lady Mansfield (1822–1870), painted 1844
3 Marianna Marchesa Florenzi, née Countess Baccinetti (1802–1870), painted 1831
4 Regina Daxenberger, married name von Fahrenbacher (1811–1872), painted 1829
5 Lady Jane Ellenborough (1807–1881), painted 1831

6 Amalie von Schintling (1812–1831), painted 1831

North wall, right

1 Mathilde Baroness von Jordan, married name Countess von Beust (1817–1886), painted 1837
2 Elise List, married name Pacher von Theinburg (1822–1893), painted 1844
3 Charlotte von Hagn, married name von Owen (1809–1891), painted 1828
4 Irene Margravine of Pallavicini, married name Countess Arco-Steppberg (1811–1877), painted 1834
5 Lady Therese Spence, née Renard (born 1815), painted 1837
6 Helene Sedlmayr, married name Miller (1813–1898), painted 1831

Amalie von Schintling, Joseph Stieler, 1831, King Ludwig I's Gallery of Beauties (Room 15)

South wall, left

1 Josepha Conti, née Reh (1822–1910), painted 1844
2 Carlotta Baroness von Breidbach-Bürresheim, married name Countess Boss-Waldeck (1838–1920), painted 1861
3 Caroline Lizius, married name Stobäus (1825–after 1904), painted 1842
4 Caroline Countess von Holnstein aus Bayern, née Baroness von Spiering (1815–1859), painted 1834
5 Lady Jane Erskine, married name Callander (1818–1846), painted 1837
6 Antonia Wallinger, married name von Ott (1823–1893), painted 1840

South wall, right

1 Creszentia Princess von Öttingen-Öttingen-Wallerstein, née Bourgin (1806–1853), painted 1833
2 Sophie Archduchess of Austria, born Princess of Bavaria, sister of King Ludwig I (1805–1872), painted 1841
3 Nanette Kaula, married name Heine (1812–1877), painted 1829

4 Catharina Botzaris, married name Karadjas (1820–1875), painted 1841
5 Friederike Baroness von Gumppenberg, married name Baroness von Gumppenberg (1823–1916), painted 1843
6 Marie, Queen of Bavaria, née Princess of Prussia, mother of King Ludwig II (1825–1889), painted 1843

Lola Montez, Joseph Stieler, 1847, King Ludwig I's Gallery of Beauties (Room 15)

West wall, left

1 Maximiliane Borzaga, married name Krämer (1806–1837), painted in 1827
2 Auguste Ferdinande Princess of Bavaria, née Archduchess of Austria, wife of Prince Regent Luitpold of Bavaria (1825–1875), painted 1845
3 Caroline Countess von Waldbott-Bassenheim, born Princess von Öttingen-Öttingen-Wallerstein (1824–1889), painted 1843
4 Alexandra Amalia Princess of Bavaria, daughter of Ludwig I (1826–1875), painted 1845
5 Lola Montez, née Gilbert (1818–1862), painted 1847
6 Maria Dietsch, married name Sprecher (1835–1869), painted 1850

West wall, right

1 Rosalie Julie Baroness von Bonar, née Baroness von Wüllersdorf-Urbair (born 1814), painted 1840
2 Amalie Baroness of Kruedener, née Countess von Lerchenfeld, later married name Countess von Adlerberg (1808–1888), painted 1828
3 Auguste Strobel, married name Hilber (1807–1871), painted 1827
4 Isabella Countess Tauffkirchen-Guttenberg-Engelburg, married name Countess Kwilecky (1808–1855), painted 1828
5 Anna Hillmayer (1812–1847), painted 1829
6 Cornelia Vetterlein, married name Baroness von Künsberg (1812–1862), painted 1828

Main palace, the queen's former study (Room 16)

16 STUDY (BURL ROOM)

This room was furnished in around 1810; the green silk wall covering was replaced when the room was restored in 1959/60. Two sopraporta paintings with Pompeian motifs.

Furnishings: On the rear wall portraits of King Ludwig I and his consort Therese, by Heinrich W. E. Vogel, 1841, after Joseph

Stieler ■ Because of the attractive alder burl veneer of the seating, the two console tables and the drawing table (probably from the workshop of the court carpenter Daniel, in 1809–1813), the former study of Queen Karoline was given the modern name Burl Room (Maserzimmer).

17 CABINET

The cabinet adjacent to the Study has delicate grotesquerie decoration by Ambrosius Hörmannstorffer dating from 1775. It was made smaller and the decoration on the south side was completed in the same style after 1900.

18 SMALL GALLERY

The south gallery continues with the Small Gallery of the south pavilion, which has a view of the Small Cascade in the cabinet garden.

Paintings: On the side walls two large still-lifes by an artist associated with Jan Fyt, mid-17th century ■ Portrait of Anna Greiner, Friedrich Dürck, 1861 ■ Portrait of Carlotta von Breidbach-Bürresheim, Friedrich Dürck, 1861.

19 AUDIENCE CHAMBER (BLUE SALON)

The blue silk covering of this salon designed by Andreas Gärtner was recreated in its original form when the room was restored in 1959/60.

Furnishings: Portraits: King Max I Joseph, Munich, c. 1810; *on the opposite side wall:* first state portrait of King Otto of Greece, Munich, 1832 ■ The console tables, commodes and seating in the Empire style (Paris, c. 1801–1807) were all part of the original furnishings. The round table with elaborate inlaid

Pharaoh busts on the round table, Paris, 1800–1805, Audience Chamber (Room 19)

Main palace, Audience Chamber (Room 19)

work and bronzes imitating the Egyptian style, on the other hand, is from Karoline's study (Paris, c. 1800–1805). ■ The two massive porcelain vases record two victories of the allies Bavaria and France. The Austerlitz vase depicts the Battle of the Three Emperors on 2 December 1805, and its counterpart shows the taking of a mountain pass near Lofer during the Bavarian-French occupation of Tyrol in November 1805 (Paris, manufactory of Pierre-Louis Dagoty, Boulevard Poissonière, 1806 or 1810).

20 BEDROOM

This room was furnished at the same time as the Audience Chamber by Andreas Gärtner and the green silk wall covering was recreated in its original form when the bedroom was restored in 1959/60. Two sopraporta paintings show Pompeian motifs.

Main palace, Bedroom (Room 20)

King Ludwig II (reigned 1864–1886) was born in this room on 25 August 1845.

Furnishings: Original Empire furnishing consisting of bed, commodes, mirror, table and seating in mahogany with bronze fittings (workshop of the court carpenter Daniel, probably by Melchior Frank, Munich, c. 1815–1817) ■ Plaster busts: Crown Prince Ludwig (II) and Prince Otto of Bavaria, Johann Halbig, modelled in 1850.

21 BATHROOM

Left: Vase with the Battle of Austerlitz, Paris, Dagoty manufactory, 1806 or 1810, Audience Chamber (Room 19)

The bathroom next to the staircase was built in 1848 by the court architect Eduard Riedel, when an apartment for King Maximilian II was being furnished in the rooms above on the 2nd floor (not accessible). The walls above the bath have been faced in deep blue stucco marble.

PALACE CHAPEL

(Entrance to the chapel in the second north pavilion from the cour d'honneur; access in the summer season during palace opening hours).

The Nymphenburg Palace Chapel in the second north pavilion

The chapel, in the "Kapellenstock" of the second north pavilion, was begun in 1702 by Antonio Viscardi from a design by Henrico Zuccalli. It is basically a rectangular room two-and-a-half floors high with a stone vault, an altar apsis on the north side, and above it a choir and organ balcony with a flat ceiling which the elector specifically requested in this form. On the first floor at the south end are balconies for the cavaliers. On the west side, above a low side aisle and extending the length of three window axes, is the elector's oratory that was the obligatory feature of court chapels, closed off by windows. Above it is a second oratory.

With the Spanish War of Succession, building was interrupted for more than a decade. Elector Max Emanuel issued an order from his place of exile that the chapel was to be finished in a simplified form by the time he returned. When it was consecrated in 1715, the room had Corinthian pilasters and simple stucco-work on the ceiling, and an elaborate stucco ceiling in the oratory on the first floor by F. Marazzi. The basic form of the high altar had been constructed, and was provisionally painted white. The present palace chapel officially took over the functions of a small chapel dedicated to Mary Magdalene located further to the south, which was already documented in the 14th century and was pulled down in 1702 when the palace was first extended (see Fig. p. 11). A few years after the consecration, the chapel walls were decorated with more elaborate stucco-work under the direction of Joseph Effner and the main altar was completed. Alterations and additions continued to be made right into the late 19th century. In 1987/91 the church was comprehensively restored, and the protective screen at the back is also from this time.

Flora basin in the Large Parterre (detail), Franz Joachim Beich, 1722/23, main palace, North Gallery, (Room 9)

The frescos on the vault are by the Tyrolean Joseph Mölck, who signed them "Joseph Mölckh Churfürstl: / Cammer = Mahler / 1759". The picture at the back shows the repentant Mary Magdalene, while the main picture illustrates the meal in the house of Simon the Pharisee. In the spandrels are representations of the Four Evangelists; the other spandrels and the lunettes are decorated with ornamental painting.

On the altar, below the combined coat of arms of Bavaria and Poland, is a carving of Christ appearing to Mary Magdalene as a gardener. This magnificent work, which in the 18th century was provisionally painted white, was finished in its present colours in around 1860. The life-sized figures, which are undoubtedly from the first third of the 17th century, are attributed to Christoph Angermair (died 1632 or 1633). Between 1750 and 1760 the richly gilded late Rococo tabernacle with reliquaries on either side was installed in front of the altar; it was probably designed by François Cuvilliés the Elder and made by artists associated with Ignaz Günther.

In the side chapel the altar retable (probably from a design by Joseph Effner) has a painting of St Hubertus by Johann Kaspar Sing. The whole altar retable was raised when the reliquary shrine with the inscription "St. PROTHI M." was added between 1735 and 1740. The reliquary is decorated with an elaborately carved gilt frame with two putti from around 1740, and from its style is probably the work of Joachim Dietrich. The large stone sculpture of St John of Nepomuk, which was initially placed in front of the Johannis Pump House by the north side wing of the palace in 1732, was transferred to the church in 1828.

COURT LIFE IN THE PALACE

The summer palace of Nymphenburg was used by the Bavarian rulers for recreational purposes and was built to accommodate the leisure pursuits of the people at court. Life at the palace was organized on a strictly hierarchichal basis.

On the main floor galleries ran through the building and served as covered corridors between the various sections. In the three middle pavilions the main floor was taken up by the electoral living quarters. Above this lived the children, court officials and servants. The ground floor of the middle section was used for sentry and supply functions. In the outer pavilion on the north side of the palace is the Court Chapel. The long subsidiary building on the north side was used for games (billiards and the ball game Pass-Spiel); and the one on the south side served first as the "Comedihaus" and orangery, and then as the kitchen. The south pavilion contained the stables for the many horses that were needed for riding and for pulling vehicles. Above these were apartments for court officials. South of this were the smithy and maintenance yard, quarters for the guards and the farm buildings. From 1730 the north pavilion housed a convent of Augustinian nuns of the Congrégation of Nôtre Dame; a small Capuchin convent which was responsible for the pastoral care of the numerous court servants had also been accommodated in this building since 1718. West of this was the extensive kitchen garden.

The Park

The park can be walked round taking the long route that is described below. This begins south of the flights of steps at the back of the palace and ends in the north by the entrance to the park. A shorter route can also be taken to visit the Amalienburg, Badenburg, Pagodenburg and Magdalenenklause, in that order. The park pavilions are described on pages 112 to 157.

The central axis of the palace park, in the foreground the Large Parterre, in the background the central canal and the Large Cascade

Previous double page: Nymphenburg Palace from the garden side, Bernardo Bellotto, known as Canaletto, 1761, Munich Residence

THE VIEW FROM THE STEPS

From the steps at the back of the palace there is a good view of the park, which is around 200 hectares (500 acres) in area, with the Large Parterre, the central canal with the Large Cascade at the end (in the direction of the Pipping church tower) and the two diagonal vistas (towards Blutenburg and Pasing) of the original Baroque garden. The axes end in ha-has, where the surrounding wall (built mainly between 1730 and 1740) was sunk, "harmoniously linking the external landscape with that of the park" (von Sckell, 1809). On either side of the central canal are the areas redesigned by Friedrich Ludwig von Sckell in the English garden style with picturesque lakes: Badenburg Lake in the southern half and Pagodenburg Lake in the northern half. On the Badenburg side a "natural" looking water course was built to flow out of the lake, with "plantings" that "overhang and adorn" it (von Sckell, 1809). The outlet from Pagodenburg Lake is an idyllic winding stream ("serpentine") that flows behind the Pagodenburg. Next to the palace on the garden side is the Large Parterre, a simplified version of the Baroque garden, with lawns edged with flowerbeds. The focal point of the view ("point de vue") from the palace is the Large Cascade (see pp. 104 to 106).

LARGE PARTERRE

Marble statue of Proserpine in the Large Parterre, Dominikus Auliczek, 1778

On the paths bordering the Parterre: statues of gods and vases in white Sterzing marble (1769 ff.): *At the corners*, marble vases decorated with putti by Roman Anton Boos, 1788–1798.
Figures along the central path: left: Cybele, the earth goddess, with mural crown and spade, by Giovanni Marchiori; *opposite:* Saturn with child, also by Marchiori (both signed OP: JOANNIS MARCHIORI on the plinth). *Left:* Jupiter with eagle and thunderbolt, from a model by Ignaz Günther, 1765; *opposite:* Juno with peacock and mirror from a model by Johann Baptist Straub, 1765; both made by Dominikus Auliczek, 1772. *Behind the basin: left:* Proserpine with sceptre and Ascalaphus as an owl; *right:* Pluto with Cerberus und fork (later erroneously completed as a trident); both from models by the court sculptor Johann Baptist Straub (1772), made by Dominikus Auliczek in 1778.
On the southern edge of the Parterre, starting at the park end and moving towards the palace: Bacchus with goblet and young satyr, by Roman Anton Boos, 1782; Venus with Cupid and apple; Mercury with staff and cockerel; both commissioned in 1773 from Ignaz Günther, produced by Roman Anton Boos, 1778.
Along the northern edge of the parterre, moving from palace to park: Diana with quiver and hound; Apollo with lyre, both by Roman Anton Boos, 1785 (Diana group signed R. A. BOOS on the dog's collar); Ceres with sheaf and sickle, by Roman Anton Boos, 1782.
The two lions on the steps with the Bavarian electoral coat of arms are by Roman Anton Boos, 1775 (replaced by copies in 1972).

SOUTH CABINET GARDEN

In the 18th century, so-called little cabinet gardens – "giardini secreti" – with a north-south axis were laid out next

South Cabinet Garden with aviary by François Cuvilliés the Elder, 1751–1757

to Zucalli's pavilions with the apartments of the elector and electress. In the south garden, which was converted into a landscape garden by Friedrich Ludwig von Sckell in the reign of Max Joseph at the beginning of the 19th century, two 18th-century constructions have been preserved: the Small Cascade and the Aviary.

Small Cascade: This was completed in 1768 by François Cuvilliés the Younger, and is probably based on an older design by Dominique Girard (1724). The Neoclassical aedicule in the background dates from the early 19th century. In the centre niche there was originally a replica of the famous Venus Italica by Antonio Canova, which is now in the Munich Residence; it has been replaced by a copy of the "Venus of Esquilin". In the side niches stone sculptures of Leda with the swan and a satyr with the boy Bacchus, both signed Konrad Eberhard, Rome, and dated 1810 and 1812, respectively. In front of the cascade a group of two figures: Diana and Endymion, both signed Konrad Eberhard, Rome 1820.

Aviary: Octagonal building which could originally be heated. With his love of exotic birds, Max III Joseph commissioned a "canary house" to be built near his apartment. The building, which was begun in 1751, was designed by François Cuvilliés the Elder and probably completed in 1757. The painting on the façade, which has been restored many times (most recently in 1974) is by Ambrosius Hörmannstorfer, who completed the gold leaf work and marbling in the Old Residence Theatre in Munich in 1753. The painting inside the Aviary, which was also his work, has been destroyed. As can be seen from the remaining fragments, there were trellises painted in the corner niches. In the middle of the room there was originally a fountain with a round basin. In 1752 the Munich court sculptor Johann Baptist Straub was paid for a lead basin with four shells, which he had completed for the Aviary. The building was altered in the early 19th century.

The ground-floor apartment of Max IV Joseph, who became King Max I, was next to the South Cabinet Garden, which was one of his favourite places. It contained rare animals and exotic plants, and he kept two black swans in the cascade basin. (The garden is not accessible).

SUMMERHOUSE IN THE CROWN PRINCE GARDEN

In around 1800, separate little gardens with summerhouses etc. were laid out near their parents' apartment and adjacent to the South Cabinet Garden for the children of the ruling family. The largest of these, the "Ludwigsgärtchen" or Crown Prince Garden, on the path to the Amalienburg, was for the future Ludwig I. The small, fenced landscape garden has a spring fed from the park canal which bubbles out of a rock, a stream and a pond. The wooden pavilion was originally known as the "Summerhouse of His Highness the Crown Prince".

The main part of the wood-framed building consists of two octagonal rooms one above the other, which are con-

nected by stairs in the projecting part of the building. The upper room has a ceiling that curves with the shallow dome of the roof – which is crowned with a half moon – and a gallery projecting from it like a balcony. The boards of the façades are painted to look like stone, and the projecting part of the building is painted to look like a brick ruin (it was thus known as the "witch's house"). It is papered inside with hand-printed wallpaper from the time it was built, which has now been restored.
The summerhouse with its two salons was probably used by the whole electoral and subsequently royal family. It was built from 1799 and resembles English summerhouses of the period, particularly with its sliding windows.
Restoration 1980/83. (The pavilion is not accessible.)

AMALIENBURG

(Text pp. 112 to 131)

FORMER MENAGERIE

The single-storey building with a mansard roof by the park wall between the Amalienburg and the Badenburg was built as a pheasantry (for golden pheasants) for Elector Max III Joseph and enlarged under King Max I for use as a menagerie, to which other buildings in the southern garden area also originally belonged. (Not accessible).

LITTLE VILLAGE WITH "GREEN PUMP HOUSE"

By the path to the Badenburg, close to the former menagerie, is a group of houses dating from the 18th century. Picturesque groups of cottages ("little villages") like this were a popular feature of Baroque gardens.
The two-storey house in the middle, the "Green Pump House" was built in 1762 and altered in 1803. Before

then, instead of the hip roof there were two high, obelisk-like water towers on top of the side tracts which became superfluous when cast iron water pipes were introduced. The building contains the pumping equipment designed by Joseph Baader in 1803/1804 and 1817 respectively, which still operates the large fountain in the garden parterre. Both machines are early technological masterpieces. They were completed by Franz Höß, who was in charge of palace fountains. On the bell-shaped air chamber of the older machine on the west side is the following inscription: MAXIMILIANI IOSEPHI IV. / ELECTORIS / IVSSV & AVSPICIIS/ construxit / IOSEPHVS BAADER / inventor / M D CCC III (1803). (The second large fountain in the crescent in front of the palace is operated by machinery in the Johannis Tower of the Orangery. Designed by Joseph Baader in 1807, installed by Franz Höß

Green Pump House with pumping equipment inside

in 1808, with the date recorded on the base. Rebuilt in 1853 by Höß in cast iron. Restored in 1974/75.)

Near the group of houses were two pools with hutches for beavers, completed in 1754 for Max III Joseph. Near the bridge over the canal are locks which were put in for the pleasure boats in the park in 1765, also during the reign of Max III Joseph.

Pan statue, Peter Lamine, 1815

Right: Monopteros on Badenburg Lake, Leo von Klenze and Carl Mühlthaler, 1862–1865

BADENBURG

(Text pp. 132 to 143)

PAN STATUE

At the east end of Badenburg Lake, by the path to the Pagodenburg, the statue of a flute-playing Pan with a goat was erected by order of King Max I Joseph on a specially sited rock with a spring rising from its base. The marble sculpture was created in 1815 by the court sculptor Peter Lamine, who had already designed a similar group in 1774 for the palace park of Schwetzingen.

MONOPTEROS

Located on a spit of land projecting from the north shore of Badenburg Lake, this building is visible from almost every part of the shore. It was preceded by a round temple made of wood, modelled on the Vesta Temple in Tivoli, with a statue of Apollo in the centre. This building was designed by Friedrich Ludwig von Sckell. On 23 February 1862, Leo von Klenze submitted a design commissioned

Large Cascade, Joseph Effner, 1717

Right: Pass-Spiel, copper engraving by Mathias Diesel, Augsburg, c. 1720

by Ludwig I for the present Monopteros, but the building, under the supervision of the court builder Carl Mühlthaler, was not actually completed until 1865. The round temple built of yellowish-grey sandstone has painted decoration in the ancient style on the frieze below the cornice and in the coffered dome. The stele in the centre is inscribed with a dedication to the patron, Ludwig I.

LARGE CASCADE

This was laid out by Joseph Effner in 1717, when Max Emanuel was still elector; the marble facing was added in 1769 under Max III Joseph. The sculptures were only assembled in their present constellation in the late 18th century, with some of the figures originating from Schleiß-

SPORT AND GAMES

At the time of Max Emanuel, the boskets north of the Large Parterre contained not only the hedge theatre and pall mall alley, but also facilities for two games. A skittle game, and in particular the Pass-Spiel were popular at the time. The latter is recorded in an illustration by the garden engineer Mathias Diesel, and the court chronicler Brétagne described the place where it was played as being bordered by two fine avenues of linden trees. According to the rules, which were drawn up by Max Emanuel himself, each player was allowed to hit one or two wooden balls with a bat across the playing area, with the aim of achieving a previously defined number of points. The players could aim either for the goals behind the barrier in the foreground or the board above the playing area. If the ball went through one of the goals or through the hole in the board, the player scored a corresponding number of points. However, if the ball rolled into one of the holes in the ground, points were deducted. The Pass-Spiel is believed to be a further development of the game of pall mall, which Max Emanuel learned in France.

heim. The reclining figures, river god and nymph, symbolizing the Danube and the Isar, are by Giuseppe Volpini, 1715–1717. The lower pair of figures, also by Giuseppe Volpini: Minerva with the owl, 1718–1721 and Hercules with the lion, 1722–1723 (replaced by copies in 1998), Flora and Aeolus, god of the winds, c. 1725; by Roman Anton Boos: Mars with sword and shield and Minerva with spear and shield – both first commissioned from Ignaz Günther; Thetis with dolphin, from a model by Charles de Groff, 1765, completed in 1775; Neptune with sea-horse, 1737, by Guillielmus de Grof.

"Iron House" after reconstruction by Carl Mühlthaler, 1867

PAGODENBURG – MAGDALENENKLAUSE

(Text pp. 144 to 151 and pp. 152 to 157) respectively

THE GLASSHOUSES

North of the Large Parterre, in separate ornamental gardens, are three glasshouses built for King Max I from plans by Friedrich Ludwig von Sckell. They reflect the growing interest in botany in the early 19th century and the king's love of tropical plants. In their time, the Nymphenburg glasshouses were the most modern in Germany, and for this reason they are of great historical value. The whole complex, with the buildings arranged in a line and the ornamental gardens in front, is an excellent example of the simple, monumental style of Neoclassical art.

The "Iron House": The first of the three glasshouses, completed in 1807. The middle section of the gallery-style building, consisting primarily of glass and iron, was originally made of wood and glass; this construction burned down in 1867. Carl Mühlthaler rebuilt the plant tract in iron and widened the northern section in the process; one of the most remarkable features of his construction is the early form of double glazing. The

"Geranium House" in Nymphenburg Palace Park

glasshouse was filled with plants from Japan, China, India, Australia, South America and Africa, and the corner pavilions contained salons for the king. The arrangement of the various sections and the decoration on the outside etc. make it more than a merely functional building. Above the west portal the inscription VERE FRVOR SEMPER / FLORAE NITIDISSIMVS HORTUS (Of veritable enjoyment forever, a luxuriant flower garden). Above the east portal: FLORAE AVSTRALI / SACRVM (Sanctum of flowers of the south) ■ Garden parterre with circular pool and fountain sculpture by Peter Lamine, 1816.

Glasshouse with a middle pavilion (today the "Geranium House"): Completed in 1816, and still in its original architectural form, it was used for growing young plants. The construction of the "light-filled plant room" is based on von Sckell's own experiments and studies. It had a glass front and the ceiling curved away from it in an arc that was continued down to the floor "so that more light can be admitted and reflected onto the plants". In front of the glasshouse a semicircular ornamental garden with four sandstone figures: the Judgement of Paris (Paris, Venus, Juno, Minerva) by Landolin Ohnmacht, Straßburg, 1804–1807. In the middle a circular pool with a fountain sculpture by Johann Nepomuk Haller from a model by Peter Lamine, 1818.

Permanent exhibition on the history of the palace park in the "Geranium House"

"Palm House": This glasshouse (now renovated and used as a café) was built in 1820 and filled mainly with palms and plants from "New Holland". In 1830 the iron stoves installed by von Sckell were replaced by the first hot water heating system in Germany. The building was completely renovated in 1965–1968, when more windows were installed on the north side and the width of the plant hall was reduced.

NORTH CABINET GARDEN

Corresponding to the garden on the south side, a cabinet garden was also laid out next to the two pavilions on the north side of the palace. This little French-style garden was originally surrounded by a pergola with marble busts on square pillars. The sculptures, which have been preserved in their original location, were probably by the court sculptors of Max Emanuel (garden not accessible).

The park pavilions

Amalienburg, view from the east

Previous double page: The central palace building viewed from the Large Cascade, in the foreground the river god "Danube", by Giuseppe Volpini, 1715–1717

To visit the Amalienburg, Badenburg, Pagodenburg and Magdalenenklause in that order, take the shorter route round the park, which follows the longer one as far as the Badenburg. From the Badenburg there is a direct connection via the central canal to the Pagodenburg.

AMALIENBURG

The Amalienburg was built in 1734–1739 during the reign of Karl Albrecht as a little hunting lodge for Electress Maria Amalia. The architect is documented as François Cuvilliés the Elder. The single-storey building has the form of a "trianon" with an oblong ground plan, in which the high central room roofed with a dome is convex on one side, while on the other side there is the suggestion of a small cour d'honneur between the building's projecting wings. The attic was originally crowned with 16 vases (from models by Johann Baptist Zimmermann), which were reconstructed in 1991. The exterior decoration is of a rather modest nature. Over the main portal a graceful group of figures with the hunting goddess Diana by Johann Baptist Zimmermann. In the round niches busts of satyrs. The interior is exceptional for the unique artistic unity of the suite of rooms and the richness of the decoration. The stucco-work is by Johann Baptist Zimmermann, the carving by Joachim Dietrich and the delicate decorative painting by Joseph Pascalin Moretti.
The almost three-dimensional figures over the main portal and on the cornice of the central hall as well as the elegant, courtly figures on the panelling of the bedroom, are

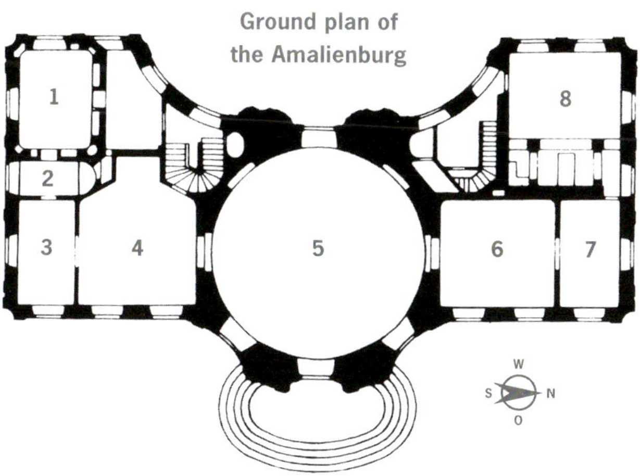

1 Dog chamber
2 "Retirade"
3 Blue Cabinet
4 Resting Room
5 Hall of Mirrors
6 Hunting Room
7 Pheasant Room
8 Kitchen

more than merely decorative. Their particular quality and a document recording that Egidius Verhelst the Elder worked from 1735–1739 on the "exquisite buildings"of Nymphenburg, indicate that Verhelst or his workshop probably "participated" in the production of the sculptures

Amalienburg, Dog Chamber (Room 1)

for the Amalienburg. It is also recorded in the archives that the Dutch sculptor and "court ornamental carver" Wolfgang Jakob Gerstens, who had already been summoned from the Netherlands during the reign of Max Emanuel, completed work "of various kinds" in the Amalienburg.

On a 1755 plan of Nymphenburg Park, the Amalienburg stands in the middle of a bosket in an open area with eight paths bordered by high hedges radiating from it. An avenue with fountains leads to the Amalienburg from the east, with a broad open avenue aligned with the large park fountain crossing it at right angles. Visitors approaching the Amalienburg did not see the whole building until they reached this point.

The delicate pink and white of the façade was restored in 1986 on the basis of findings and corresponds to the original colours of 1736. The apparent reversal of the colours between the outer and central risalits is consistent with the construction of the walls, but is nevertheless a particularly attractive feature designed by Cuvilliés to appeal to visitors as they emerged from the corridors of hedges. The original colours of the interior, which were uncovered during the restoration in 1956/58, correspond to the colour scheme on the ground-plan of the Amalienburg by François Cuvilliés the Younger dating from 1771. According to this, the silvered decoration in the Hall of Mirrors was on a white background ("à fond Blanc"): this is evidently a reference to the decoration on the cupola which is the dominant feature of the room. For the Resting Room and the Hunting Room, "yellow" is given as the basic colour, in two shades: straw ("fond Couleur de Paille") and lemon ("fond Citron"). The Amalienburg was restored for the first time in 1769, under Max III Joseph, with the participation of the court stucco-worker Franz Xaver Feichtmayr the Younger.

1 DOG CHAMBER

The walls and ceilings of the panelled room with recesses for the dogs and gun cupboards are decorated to look like Dutch tiles with blue Camaieu painting in the "Chinese" style by Joseph Pascalin Moretti. Between the flowers and fruits of the early Rococo decoration are numerous hunting motifs, including the owl as a decoy bird. Over the doors are roebuck and fox hunts (a dog with the monogramme CA= Carl Albrecht). In the window-jambs delicately painted landscapes with motifs from the Nymphenburg hunting grounds have been preserved in their original form. The rounded corner of the room conceals a stove.

Amalienburg, Resting Room (Room 4), carved wall panelling

2 "RETIRADE"

Panelling with blue-and-white decoration alternates with still-lifes of flowers with animals by Franz de Hamilton and Arcadian landscapes. The rear wall is designed to look like a commode, and has a toilet chair concealed behind its folding doors. In the niche and on the ceiling decorative painting by Joseph Pascalin Moretti.

3 BLUE CABINET

The corner room of this magnificent suite of residential rooms has elegantly carved ornamentation in silver on the base section of the wall, door panels and shutters, silver stucco-work on the ceiling and beautifully carved hunting trophies on the wings of the door to the Resting Room.

Furnishings: Two tabourets and a Venetian glass chandelier from the time the Amalienburg was built ■ Light-blue damask wall covering last replaced in 1990, as were also the curtains.

4 RESTING ROOM

The walls are richly decorated in yellow ("fond Citron") and silver. The carving with its hunting motifs on the panelled walls – one of the most exquisite examples of Rococo decoration – flows into the stucco-work decora-

tion of the ceiling. The carved figures on the rear wall of the bed alcove are exceptionally beautiful. On either side of the bed alcove portraits of Elector Karl Albrecht and Maria Amalia in hunting dress from the atelier of George Desmarées.

Furnishings: Console table in the shape of a chest, Joachim Dietrich from a design by François Cuvilliés the Elder, 1735–1739 ■ Here, as in the following rooms, Venetian chandeliers which were part of the original decor ■ Originally the mantelpiece was decorated with a clock with a pagod (with the name of Gudin le jeune on the mechanism) and candelabra with Fo gods in "blanc de chine" on silver-bronze stands (inventory of 1763, currently in storage). ■ Daybed "lit en niche" and curtains reconstructed in 1991 in a slightly simplified form, based on the inventory description of 1758.

Amalienburg, Resting Room (Room 4)

Next double page: Amalienburg, Hall of Mirrors (Room 5)

5 HALL OF MIRRORS

With its unique decoration in silvered stucco this hall, which is circular with a flat cupola, is the highpoint of the palace's interior. The classical forms (pilasters, columns, pillars) previously used to structure a room have now been replaced by rocaille decoration. Windows and mirrors alternate round the walls, which brings the world of the garden inside. The themes of the ceiling stucco-work with the four figures of Diana, Amphitrite, Ceres and Bacchus, are hunting and the pleasures of the table. The room was used for banquets, balls, concerts and relaxation after the hunt.

Furniture: Richly carved, silvered console tables, Joachim Dietrich from a design by François Cuvilliés the Elder, 1735–1739, with rich shell ornamentation (rocailles) and silvered tabourets, possibly Wolfgang Jakob Gerstens from a design by François Cuvilliés the Elder, 1738–1739.

6 HUNTING ROOM

The walls are decorated in silver and yellow ("couleur de Paille"). The room, which could be heated by an open fire, is designed as a small gallery, with the paintings arranged one above the other as was the custom in the 18th century.

Amalienburg, Hunting Room (Room 6)

List of paintings, from left to right:

BOTTOM ROW:
Fireplace wall: Seine landscape with a view of Saint-Cloud ■ Seine landscape with the garden parterre of the electoral palace of Saint-Cloud. Both painted by Jean Baptiste Feret, c. 1714, in memory of Elector Max Emanuel's exile. Originally in the small gallery of the first north pavilion in the main palace.
Exit wall (north side): River landscape with wild animals ■ River landscape with birds, both paintings in the style of Franz de Hamilton.
Exit wall (south side): River landscape with many different kinds of birds ■ Hilly landscape with stags and hares, both in the style of Franz de Hamilton.

IN THE TOP ROW:
The top row of paintings is a series of six illustrations of court festivals and hunting from the reign of Elector Karl Albrecht, when the little palace was built. They are some of the first works commissioned by the elector from Peter Jakob Horemans (1700–1775) of Antwerp. Five of the pictures were specially painted for the Amalienburg when it was built in 1734–1739. The sixth – Falconry by the aviary – was added shortly after 1770. According to Horemans himself, in the six paintings "in Amalienburg over 200 portraits" can be seen.
Fireplace wall:
Round races at the elector's court at Fürstenried Palace.
Painted in 1732. The event depicted was part of the festivities marking the birth of the heir Maximilian Joseph and the ac-

cession to power of Karl Albrecht in the spring of 1727: "On 14 May at the Electoral summer residence and hunting lodge of Fürstenried a peasant wedding was staged by Their Highnesses the Electoral family and members of the high nobility, followed by a tournament in which Her Highness the Electress and Her Highness the Duchess [Maria Anna], and other ladies took part, in fine new carriages specially made for the occasion. Both Their Highnesses were driven by Their Highnesses the Elector and Duke Ferdinand, the others by the cavaliers, and Her Highness the Electress won the contest with the lance".

In the carriage drawn by two horses in the foreground sits Electress Maria Amalia, driven by Elector Karl Albrecht. A cavalier bears a pole on which is the head of a Turk as a trophy. On the left next to them Duke Ferdinand Maria and Maria Anna of Bavaria. In the background architecture in the form of a triumphal arch erected for the festivities, and behind this Fürstenried Palace. The ladies wore "Roman" dress for the round race. Steered round the race course by cavaliers, they had to hit the heart of a cupid with lances and darts, wound a chicken that lay in the mouth of a fox with daggers, and hit with a ball the shield held by a figure. The winners were rewarded with various prizes.

Elector Karl Albrecht at a "German hunt" by the "Red House", Peter Jakob Horemans, 1739, Hunting Room (Room 6)

Tournament races on stags near Allach at the so-called Green House.

Painted in 1734. Festivities on 15 May 1727: "On 15 May, when the esteemed magistrate and citizenry of the residency of Munich came to pay homage, a tournament on live animals was held between two small woods between Nymphenburg, Allach and Mosen ... whereby His Highness the Elector had the best results in the dagger and pour la Dame contests; His Highness Duke Ferdinand won the arrow contest, and His Highness Duke Theodor the lance contest."

The rider on the white horse in the foreground is possibly Johann Theodor, Prince-Bishop of Freising. At the tournament red and fallow deer were driven into elongated enclosures and brought down as the riders went by with lances, darts, daggers and pistols. In the background, as in the previous picture, festival architecture in the form of triumphal arches. The "Green House" was one of the electoral hunting lodges between Moosach and Untermenzing.

Elector Karl Albrecht and Electress Maria Amalia with courtiers engaged in falconry at the so-called aviary, Peter Jakob Horemans, 1770, Hunting Room (Room 6)

Exit wall (north side):
Riding to the hounds under Elector Karl Albrecht at the "Yellow House" near Fürstenried Palace.
Painted in 1736. In the middle is Karl Albrecht on a light-coloured horse. On his right Elector Clemens August of Cologne. On his left probably Ferdinand Maria and Johann Theodor, the other brothers. In the background the "Yellow House", a hunting lodge built in the form of a miniature palace in 1734, and described by the Bamberg architect J. M. Küchel as follows: "This yellow house has 4 pavilions, with rooms in 3 of them and the stairs in the 4th, and in the middle an octagonal hall; upstairs are 6 rooms. The whole building is of wood and all the rooms are wallpapered, every one in a different paper, and from every window there is a view of an avenue, which is at least an hour's journey long; this little building is altogether very pretty ..."

Elector Karl Albrecht changes his boots at the "Blue House" after a fall.
Painted in 1738. The incident took place on 26 November 1734 in Forstenried Park. The elector fell off his horse and into the water while pursuing a wild boar over the River Würm. He took off his heavy riding boots to wade across the river and rode barefoot to the "Blue House", where he put on dry boots and clothing.
In the centre of the picture is the elector with servants. Also depicted are Duke Johann Theodor and the seven-year-old electoral prince Max Joseph. In the middle distance to the right, Electress Maria Amalia is getting into a coach and nearby Elector Clemens August of Cologne is also changing his

boots. The "Blue House" was around an hour south of Maria Eich near Planegg.

Entrance wall (south side):
Elector Karl Albrecht and Electress Maria Amalia with courtiers engaged in falconry at the so-called aviary.
Painted in 1770. The hunt in question took place on 29 June 1741. In the centre of the group is Elector Karl Albrecht, on the right the electress and behind her Duke Ferdinand Maria. Left of Karl Albrecht is the electoral prince Max Joseph, further to the left, with a light-coloured falcon on his hand, Elector Clemens August of Cologne. The aviary was one of the permanent hunting facilities, and was located, judging by the silhouette of Munich in the background, near Nymphenburg Palace.

Elector Karl Albrecht at a "German hunt" by the "Red House".
Painted in 1739. "German hunting" involved the pursuit on horseback of bears or fierce wild boars. The animals were caught by the pack of dogs and then killed by the hunter.
In the centre of the picture Karl Albrecht is depicted on horseback, in the process of killing the boar cornered by the dogs with his dagger. The elector is surrounded by members of his family. Behind a group of riders to the right is the electress in a coach. The "Red House" was located south-west of Pasing on the River Würm.

WINDOW PILLAR:
Four paintings one above the other: hunting animals and still life pictures of game.
Furnishings: Chest, Joachim Dietrich from a design by François Cuvilliés the Elder, 1735–1739 ■ Silvered tabourets covered in brocade interwoven with silver thread, from the original furnishings ■ Above the fireplace a valuable wall clock by the Parisian clockmaker C.P. G. Mesnil made of Chinese porcelain from the K'ang-hsi-period with Meissen flowers (currently in storage).

7 PHEASANT ROOM OR "INDIAN CABINET"

Counterpart of the Blue Cabinet. The large wooden panels on the walls are covered with coarse, glue-primed linen decorated with multicoloured ornamental painting interspersed with pheasants on a light-blue background, in imitation of Chinese textile wall coverings. The motifs were originally outlined in gold and silver, but only fragments of this metalwork have remained, and the colours have largely faded.

As the writing cabinet of Maria Amalia, which had a lacquered, "pearl-coloured" writing table with silver fittings, this, the smallest room in the building, was originally the most colourful of them all. On the ceiling silvered stuccowork.

8 KITCHEN

The lavish artistic decoration makes this kitchen quite unique. The walls are covered with blue-and-white and coloured Dutch tiles, the coloured tiles assembled to depict magnificent vases of flowers and everyday life in China in the style of Chinese vase painting. The ceiling and wooden panelling is painted with blue and white chinoiseries by Joseph Pascalin Moretti.

The tiles forming the three multicoloured flower vase pictures are probably from the "Rose" manufactory in Delft. The motif is almost identical with four multicoloured floor vases from the same manufactory in a ground-floor room in Rambouillet Palace in France. This room, which was lined entirely with Dutch tiles, was created in 1715–1730 and was probably used by the Comtesse de Toulouse as a dining room. In the Amalienburg, some of the tiles forming the rare multicoloured pictures of Chinese scenes were laid in the wrong place. The blue-and-white tiles have the usual Biblical, mythological

Amalienburg, Kitchen (Room 8), ceiling painting with chinoiseries by Joseph Pascalin Moretti

Right: Amalienburg, Kitchen (Room 8)

and landscape motifs. The walls are structured with a manganese-coloured motif of twisted, garlanded pillars. The magnificent decoration of the room, situated right next to the private writing cabinet of the electress rather than in the cellar or the subsidiary building that once stood on the south side of the Amalienburg, probably derives from the fact that "the electress herself loved to cook here", as the children Nannerl and Wolfgang Amadeus Mozart were told when they visited the Amalienburg in 1763.

BADENBURG

Opposite the Pagodenburg in the south part of the park is the Badenburg, which was already being admired in its day as a “chef d’oeuvre de l’art” (Brétagne, 1722). The original little bathing palace was the idea of Elector Max Emanuel, and it was built for him in 1718–1721 by Joseph Effner. The form and use of the Badenburg was influenced by the bathing houses he had seen shortly beforehand during his exile in France. Modern bathing facilities had become considerably more important in France in around 1700, a development that had originated with the royal baths, the bathing apartment of Louis XIV in Versailles and the “Pavillon des Bains” in the summer palace of Marly. The ground-plan of the two-storey building is dominated by the great hall which projects from the rest of the building on the entrance side. Adjacent to it on the south side is a rectangular wing with a residential apartment and a bathing hall, which is carried through two floors (the basement and the ground floor). The main façade was originally decorated with stucco-work by the French sculptor and stucco-worker Charles Dubut; the attic was crowned with lead vases. In front of the little palace, as part of the geometric garden and to set the scene for the bathhouse, Effner laid out a terrace with a large basin and numerous fountains, while the south side had a flower parterre. The surroundings of the Badenburg were altered completely by Friedrich Ludwig von Sckell, who transformed the bosket garden into a landscape garden through the creation of a “natural” lake and the “Lion Valley” (named after the two lions made by Charles de Groff in 1769 for the south steps of the Badenburg), and the building then became a decorative architectural feature instead of a focal point of the garden. In the early 19th century, Leo von Klenze gave the pavilion a rather more austere appearance in the Neoclassical style by removing the stucco-work.

Badenburg, view from the north

Ground plan of the Badenburg

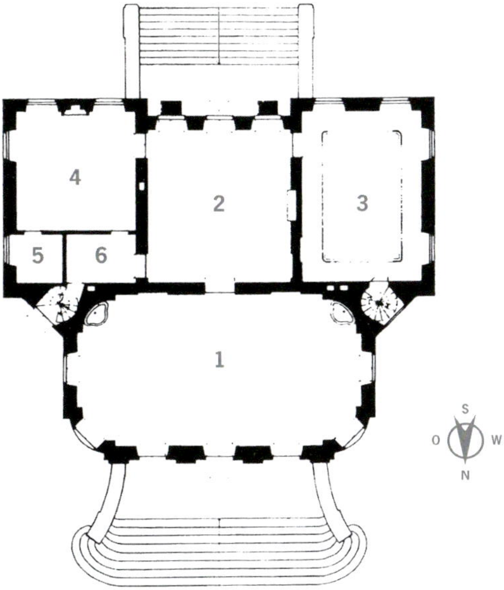

1 Great Hall
2 Antechamber
3 Bathing Hall
4 Bedroom
5 Singerie Cabinet
6 Former cloakroom

After the bomb damage from the last war had been repaired, from 1975–1980 the Badenburg was comprehensively restored. The ceiling picture in the hall by Jacopo Amigoni had been almost completely destroyed, with only fragments of the figures at its edges remaining. The restoration was based on the colours of the remaining fragments and a coloured photo. The interior of the Badenburg has regained its original appearance in particular through the rediscovery of the historical Chinese wallpaper: this now once again decorates the living quarters after having either been uncovered or brought out of storage. All the wallpaper was restored in 1985–1988 and most recently in 2007.

Badenburg, Great Hall (Room 1)

1 GREAT HALL

The two-storey hall is dominated by round-arched glass doors with oval windows set in the wall above them. With its white stucco-work, ceiling fresco and marble floor it is designed as a garden hall. The ceiling picture (reconstruction by Karl Manninger, 1984) shows the rising sun god in association with morning, spring and water. The scene is surrounded by spring nymphs and river gods in a setting of rocks and reeds. It is a reference to the onset of the warm season, the time when the court was able to use the garden palace. The walls are decorated with lavish stucco-work with flower garlands and four putto groups representing the seasons. Realistic baskets of fruit, sheaves of corn and bunches of grapes overflowing the cornice present themselves to view from the doorway. Musical instruments also feature, and the decor in the late Baroque style is a splendid synthesis of the themes of music, the pleasures of the table and the element of water. Water is not only symbolized but is also a physical element of the design: in the corners of the room are red marble fountain shells for cooling wine, each with two Triton children in gilt lead made by Guillielmus de Grof in 1722.

2 ANTECHAMBER

Badenburg, Bathing Hall (Room 3)

The Antechamber marks the beginning of the private apartment, and also provides access to the spectators' balcony of the bathroom. All the rooms of this apartment, which was completed between 1721 and 1724, have typical Baroque interiors with panelling on the base section of the wall and a cornice. The area in between was originally decorated with precious Chinese wall coverings; these textiles were however vulnerable to light and did not last. The present red wallpaper from China was put up for King Max I Joseph in around 1806 and was probably made at the end of the 18th century. Against what was originally a bright red background, it depicts a flower garden in green and silver with exotic insects and birds. Bright colours were popular in the Neoclassical era. After 200 years of exposure to light, the once vivid colours have faded.
The white painting of the wooden areas is original; the panelling in the hall and the bedroom was also once painted white. Max Emanuel originally had an important painting – Sébastien Bourdon's "Perseus and Andromeda" – hung over the fireplace. The story, which is associated with the legendary origin of coral, also fits in with the sea mythology of the building. In 1791 the picture was taken to the Hofgarten Gallery in Munich and it now hangs in the Alte Pinakothek. Today in its place there is a picture of a white fox shot in the electoral hunting revier of Kling on 9.10.1777, painted by Joseph Stephan.

3 BATHING HALL

The magnificent Bathing Hall is unusually large for the time when it was built. The bath itself is in the basement, and the lower part was originally faced with lead. The walls above water-level are decorated with blue-and-white "Dutch" tiles. Stucco consoles in the shape of busts, the

Badenburg, Bedroom (Room 4)

lower part of which has been restored, support the gallery surrounding the upper section of the room. The walls are covered with magnificent black and reddish stucco marble with agate-coloured relief sections by the Bavarian stucco-worker Johann Georg Bader. The stucco-work on the cornice was already being renovated by Johann Baptist Zimmermann in 1736. In the wrought-iron railing by the court

ornamental metalworker, Antoine Motté, is the electoral crown and the monogramme of Max Emanuel (ME), for whom the Badenburg was built. The decorative, delicately-tinted ceiling painting (oil on canvas, cleaned and restored in 1952), is by the French artist Nicolas Bertin. It was made in Paris and rolled up for transportation to Munich. The painting (a grisaille) depicts fountains and mythological scenes revolving around the theme of bathing: Hercules hurling a rock at the water nymphs; Diana bathing; Leda with the swan; Europa swimming the Hellespont on the bull.
The bath was entered by a small staircase with tiled walls. The heating system in the basement with a walled-in stove and twisted pipes in the boiler is still in place. The basement rooms included two small bathing apartments each with a bath-tub and a quiet room as well as a kitchen with an open fireplace (not accessible).

4 BEDROOM

The present wallpaper in the bedroom was hung shortly after 1806 when Max I Joseph had the Badenburg renovated. It is a high quality export product for Europe, which depicts scenes from Chinese life. The main scene shows a high imperial official with his favourite wife, his family and his servants. The falcon perched on a rock next to him is waiting for the hunt to commence. In the background is a panoramic landscape with a hint of linear perspective – a stylistic concession to European conventions. Until 1806, Max Emanuel's bed with a baldachin "à l'imperiale" stood against the back wall of the room. Its hangings were made of a cotton material called "Pers" with an Indian-style flower pattern in red and white. The bed was an important element of the exotic room decoration.
The south side has oak boiserie from the time the Badenburg was built, one of the most elegant, confidently executed examples of interior decoration completed for Max

Emanuel. It was probably based on a French design, as not only the quality of the carving suggests. The gilt mirror frame over the fireplace with Neptune masks spouting water and mythological beasts from the Pichler workshop looks much less sophisticated by comparison.

Badenburg, Singerie Cabinet (Room 5), ceiling painting with monkey as bonvivant

Right: Badenburg, Singerie Cabinet (Room 5)

5 SINGERIE CABINET

The toilette and writing cabinet is the most intimate and precious room in this apartment. It was the first silvered room at the Munich court and is the only room in the Badenburg where the original furniture has been preserved. The yellow leather coverings of the carved, silvered set of table, barber chair and two tabourets have been replaced. They matched the original silk wallpaper: the whole cabinet was in silver, white and yellow. The canvas ceiling painting (probably from a design by Effner, around 1720) gives the room its playful, ironic character. It is bordered with arabesque ornamentation consisting of strapwork and latticework, and features eight monkeys grouped around a star motif. Singeries like this were popular at the time, and here they are part of the exotic iconography of the Badenburg as a whole. In imitation of human beings, they are occupying themselves with varying degrees of seriousness with the arts and sciences:

Ceiling painting: East side: Monkey with books; *South-east side:* Monkey as a mathematician with a sheet of calculations; *South side:* Monkey with building plans and angle measure; *South-west side:* Monkey with globe; *West side:* Monkey with

Ceiling painting, c. 1720, Badenburg, Singerie Cabinet (Room 5)

paintbrush, palette and picture of an owl; *North-west side:* Monkey as bonvivant with wine glass and roast meat; *North side:* Monkey with sculptor's tools; *North-east side:* Monkey with bagpipes.

The missing 18th-century silk wall covering painted with life-size Chinese figures probably added to the entertaining quality of the room. Today it has been replaced by wallpaper purchased in the second half of the 18th century. The high-quality Chinese export shows everyday rural scenes peopled with small figures.

6 FORMER CLOAKROOM

In the 1980s, wallpaper of an older date was discovered beneath the wallpaper in the bedroom, which had been stuck over it in around 1806. It must have been hung between 1751 and 1763 in the reign of Max III Joseph to replace the silk covering of Max Emanuel's time and is one of the oldest examples of Chinese wallpaper to have been preserved. Following its restoration, this valuable wall covering now hangs in the cloakroom. It consists of large individual woodcuts which were stuck together on the wall. For this reason the motifs are repeated. The woodcuts may have been New Year prints which were hung up in China for the New Year festival and were supposed to bring luck. The doll-like ladies on the seat probably symbolize riches and nobility, the boys at play posterity. After the paper was put up in the Badenburg, an artist painted over the joins with twining plants and animals.

Chinese wallpaper, Badenburg, Former cloakroom (Room 6)

From the cloakroom, which was next to the bedroom, there was direct access to the bath in the cellar via a spiral staircase.

On the upper floor of the Badenburg there were a few comfortably furnished rooms for the members of the elector's closest retinue. These were partially restored after destruction in the Second World War (not accessible).

PAGODENBURG

Pagodenburg, view from the south-west

The architect of the elegant, two-storey building constructed in 1716–1719 was Joseph Effner. According to tradition, however, the imaginative ground-plan, an octagon eight-metres across which is extended with cruciform arms, was the work of Max Emanuel himself. This outline is probably based on French models, such as the "Pavillon du soleil" in Marly, and more especially the octagonal hunting lodge built for Max Emanuel in Bouchefort near Brussels by Germain Boffrand. It also however bears an interesting resemblance to Turkish seraglios, which Europeans were familiar with from engravings. While the exterior has nothing Asian about it, in the rich decoration of the interior, Turkish and Far-Eastern motifs blend seamlessly to create the exotic atmosphere that had just become fashionable but rarely succeeded as it does here. The name of this little palace is said to have originated from its painted decoration "with Chinese figures like pagods" (idols).

The exterior is decorated with pilasters with Corinthian capitals. The ornamentation on the windows and balconies is mainly a Rococo version of the original motifs, produced during a general renovation under François Cuvilliés the Elder in around 1767/68. The present pale grey, beige and white colour scheme also dates back to this time. The surfaces of the attic wall concealing the flat, tented roof were originally decorated with ornamental painting and there were balustrades and ornamental vases on top, which gave the building a more whimsical character.

The balconies in French wrought-iron technique are by Antoine Motté, with "fleurons de bronze" by Guillielmus de Grof. Over the entrance and the windows of the lower floors are sculptured masks representing Bacchus, Flora, Neptune und Ceres.

Ground plan of the Pagodenburg

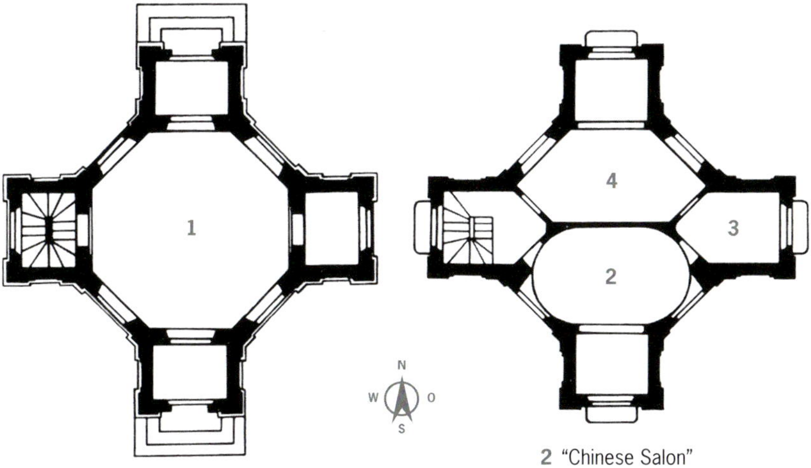

1 Small Hall ("Saletl")

2 "Chinese Salon"
3 "Chinese Cabinet"
4 Resting Room

Pagodenburg, Small Hall (Room 1)

The little garden pavilion was used for intimate parties where the strict formalities of court ceremonies could be relaxed, and where, in particular, players could rest from the exertions of pall mall, a game akin to bowls for which a horse-shoe shaped alley had been created on the north side of the Pagodenburg (today Pagodenburg Valley).
The architecture of the Pagodenburg was reproduced in a garden pavilion in the Baden Residence of Rastatt: Margravine Sibylla Augusta sent for copies of the plans from Munich in 1772 and built her own "Pagodenburg", though with a different roof.

In 1961/63 the Small Hall ("Saletl") was restored and the cavettos, which had been painted over in the 19th century, were restored to their original condition. The stucco decoration here was produced using the "combined technique": part of the decoration was applied directly and part made in the workshop and appled in completed form. The original glazed blue and silver of the wooden framework was uncovered. The last comprehensive external and internal restoration took place from 1995 to 2004.

1 GROUND FLOOR WITH HALL AND STAIRCASE

On the ground floor the rooms are arranged in accordance with the ground-plan, with four cabinet-like, rectangular side rooms added on to the small octagonal hall, the Small Hall ("Saletl", Room 1). Round the edge of the ornamental ceiling painting (Johann Anton Gumpp, 1718/19) in the central room are the Four Continents and busts of mythological figures on pedestals. The ceiling painting of the entrance room features Bacchus, that of the cabinet opposite Venus, while the ceiling in the cabinet on the east side has Bacchanalian scenes on a gold background. The paintings here and on the ceilings of the upper floors are almost all probably true copies made after 1870. As in the upper cabinets, the stucco strapwork and latticework on the cornices was evidently produced by the workshop of Guillielmus de Grof, which is documented as having completed the stucco-work in the "Cabinet next to the bowling alley". In the absence of porcelain from Eastern Asia, and with European porcelain in its early days, Max Emanuel selected Dutch faience tiles for the walls of the ground floor and the stairwell, to create an exotic, Chinese atmosphere.
The almost 2000 beautifully painted Dutch tiles are decorated with a variety of landscapes and figures and are probably from Rotterdam. On the upper floor are two tile

Pagodenburg, "Chinese Salon" (Room 2)

paintings depicting a French garden. The arrangement of the tiles is similar to that of the above-mentioned (cf. Amalienburg kitchen) tiled ground-floor room in Rambouillet Palace, which has two blue-and-white tile paintings of Amsterdam and Rotterdam signed by the Rotterdam faience painter Cornelis Boumeester. The matching blue-and-white tiles covering the rest of the wall are from a Rotterdam manufactory.

Not only the tile paintings but also the ceiling painting, the stucco-work on the walls, the tiled boiseries and the furniture are in blue and white, to emphasize the Far-Eastern character of the interior.

The present furnishings date from the renovation period under Elector Max III Joseph: Large round table with a carved stand and four sofas in blue and white, c. 1770 ■ Eight-armed carved chandelier, painted blue and white to look like porcelain, by Johann Thomas Sailler, 1762 ■ Two landscape paintings by Pieter Rysbraeck (1655–1729).

2 – 4 UPPER FLOOR

The ingenious arrangement of the rooms on the upper floor comes as a surprise, and underlines the graceful character of the building. Two of the cabinets ("Chinese Salon", Room 2; "Chinese Cabinet", Room 3) have interiors in the Eastern-Asian style, decorated with Chinese wallpaper painted with colourful flowers and birds which is set into black-and-red lacquer panels. This wallpaper was most certainly purchased by Max Emanuel in Paris; the framework system was based on the structure of Chinese screens. The frequently restored ceiling paintings with the "pagods" are by Johann Anton Gumpp. Exquisite Parisian furniture completed the interior, most of which has been preserved. From the furniture it can be seen that the Chinese fashion introduced under Max Emanuel was copied from the French court.

The elector had precious furniture with Japanese lacquer panels purchased in Paris. The lacquer commode in the "Chinese Salon" is one of the oldest examples of the transformation of a Japanese lacquered chest into an item of European furniture such as a commode (Paris, c. 1715/20; lacquer: Japan, c. 1660–1690, conifer wood, willow, urushi lacquer, bronze – its counterpart is on display in the Badenburg.)

Lacquer commode, Paris, c. 1715/20, "Chinese Salon" (Room 2)

Pagodenburg, "Chinese Cabinet" (Room 3)

Right: Pagodenburg, Resting Room (Room 4)

Other furniture: Ebony games table with an inlaid chess board, probably Master "FL", alias François Lieutaud, Paris, c. 1720 ■ The apartment is furnished with two sets of tabourets of exceptionally high quality, designed by Joseph Effner, Munich, c. 1718/19.

Only the third room (Resting Room, Room 4) has gold-and-white Régence panelling. The alcove walls are covered with very rare red-and-green Genoese silk brocade (so-called velours "jardinière"). The two daybeds and seating, which were part of the original furnishings, are covered in the same material.

MAGDALENENKLAUSE

Magdalenen-klause, View from the south

The hermitage, designed as an artificial ruin with an interior consisting of a grotto and four adjoining, simple, cell-like rooms was built by Joseph Effner towards the end of Max Emanuel's reign (from 1725). It is an example of a rather strange type of building that was found in palace gardens in the late 17th and 18th centuries and expressed the idea of escape from court ceremony into solitude for religious and philosophical meditation, the enjoyment of simplicity and the peaceful appreciation of nature. These deliberately designed ruins "whose appearance indicates poverty", imitate the half-ruined huts of hermits. The Magdalenenklause is the court counterpart of the hermitages frequently built in monasteries from the 17th century on. Another interesting feature here is the use at this early stage of historicizing architectural details (Romanesque, Gothic and Moorish).

In accordance with building's purpose as a place for prayer and monastic living, the rectangular, single-storey building is divided into a chapel and four adjoining residential rooms; there are two apses opposite one another on the short sides (one for the altar and one for the bed alcove), and on two of the corners are low rounded oriels. The altar apsis is decorated with Moorish-style windows. Above the entrance on the east side is a Baroque gable, which is designed in the Italian style as an open belfry. The building originally looked much more like a ruin, as the walls were higher in places, but the roof was almost all lower. In 1750, because of frequent complaints that it let in the water, Max III Joseph had the building covered with the present hip roof, and the lantern of the chapel vault scarcely rises above it.

Over the entrance with its wrought-iron doors by Antoine Motté (1726) is a marble slab with an inscription recording the consecration of the chapel by the Archbishop and Elector of Cologne, Clemens August, on 4 April, 1728.

Ground plan of the Magdalenenklause

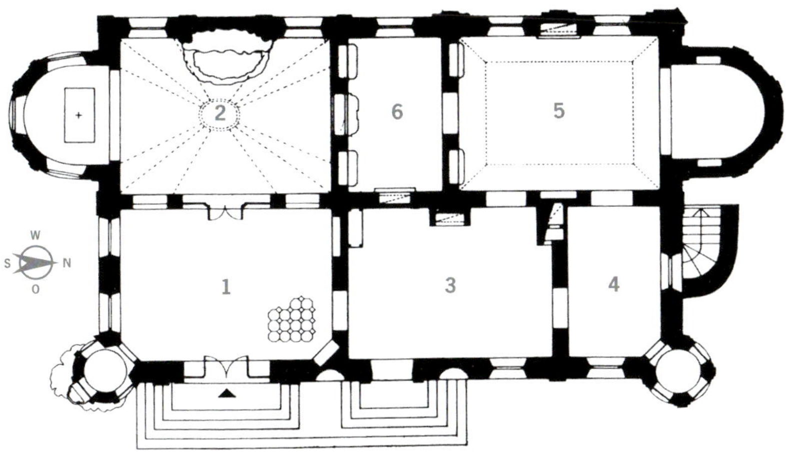

1 Vestibule
2 Chapel of St Mary Magdalene
3 Anteroom
4 Cabinet
5 Refectory (former Bedroom)
6 Oratory

The chapel takes up almost half the building. It is divided by two pillars into an anteroom (Room 1) and the chapel proper (Room 2). Both rooms are designed as a grotto: the walls are faced with tuff which has artificial coral sprouting from it, and with grotto work (stucco-work with shells, coloured pebbles, stucco birds etc.) The grotto work was completed by Johann Bernhard Joch from Munich in 1726. As the fragments of paint show, it was all once very colourful. The wrought-iron entrance to the chapel is by the French ornamental metalworker Antoine Motté. In the round room at the outer corner of the anteroom is a well shaft, from which a fountain basin outside can also be fed.

Magdalenenklause, Chapel with altar (Room 2)

The chapel ceiling is a trough vault set with coloured stones as in a mosaic, with painted areas showing scenes from the life of the repentant Mary Magdalene by the artist Nikolaus Gottfried Stuber. The dome opens in a round lantern, which is also encrusted with coloured grotto stones. On the outer wall opposite the entrance is a grotto niche with a stucco figure of St Mary Magdalene by Giuseppe Volpini, 1726. Beneath it is a basin of natural rock with water popularly believed to have healing properties for eyes, but which is in fact diverted from the park canal close to and at a higher level than the hermitage. The wooden altar, which significantly faces not the entrance but the elector's rooms, has an antependium inlaid in walnut and maple by the Nymphenburg court cabinet maker Johann Michael Höcker. The crucifix and candelabra, made rather unusually of narwhal tusk, are in keeping with the character of the hermitage. The two boxwood reliefs are inscribed "Ignatius Hyllebrand, Bildhauer [sculptor] in Türkheim 1760".

The four rooms – Anteroom, Cabinet, Refectory with alcove and Oratory (Rooms 3 to 6) – are uniformly panelled in simple stained oak with profiled centre sections. The original heating system is still in place with a tiled stove which heats three rooms at once and the various components of the system concealed behind the panelling of the anteroom. The tiles are a different colour in every room (blue, black, green) and decorated with a variety of motifs.

In the former bed alcove, which matches the chapel apse on the opposite side of the building, hangs a Serbian-Byzantine cross, and in the same room there is a turned olive-wood chandelier. In the base section of the wall below the window facing the chapel in the last room is a prie-dieu, so that Max Emanuel could watch the service from here. The oil paintings (George Desmarées, St Karl Borromeus, 1739; Repentant Mary Magdalene, Italy, 17th century), the drawings (eight pen and ink drawings of the Passion of Christ by Christoph Schwarz, from 1589), the engravings (including a hermit series by Jan Sadeler) and the symbolic representations of the Four Last Things, modelled in wax (first half of the 18th century) are all part of the original furnishings.

In the 18th century the majolica dinner service of Duke Albrecht V (Faenza, Don Pino, 1576) was used here (today in the Munich Residence Museum). According to the old palace inventories, the service with the coat of arms of the Bavarian dukes was kept in

Wickerwork armchair, Paris, c. 1725/26, Magdalenenklause

Magdalenenklause, Refectory with former bed alcove (Room 5)

large cupboards in the cellar of the Magdalenenenklause, where there was also a kitchen. In the glass cases Chinese and Japanese porcelain, 17th/18th century (K'ang-hsi and Imari).

Furniture: The unpainted wickerwork furniture (three armchairs, 12 chairs, Paris, c. 1725/26) are part of the original furnishings. The armchairs were placed at the desks built into the walls and at wall tables (Munich, 1727–1728).

The rulers

ELECTOR FERDINAND MARIA (1636–1679)
Reigned 1651–1679
Married 1652 to Adelaide (Adelheid Henriette Maria), daughter of Duke Victor Amadeus I of Savoy

Elector Karl Theodor (detail), Pompeo Batoni, c. 1775/90, Munich Residence

ELECTOR MAX EMANUEL (1662–1726)
Reigned 1680–1726
First marriage in 1685 to Maria Antonia, daughter of Emperor Leopold I
Second marriage in 1695 to Therese Kunigunde, daughter of King Johann III Sobieski of Poland

ELECTOR KARL ALBRECHT (1697–1745)
Reigned 1726–1745, crowned Emperor Karl VII, 1742
Married 1722 to Maria Amalia Josepha, daughter of Emperor Joseph I

ELECTOR MAX III JOSEPH (1727–1777)
Reigned 1745–1777
Married 1747 to Maria Anna Sophie, daughter of King Friedrich August III of Poland and Elector of Saxony

ELECTOR KARL THEODOR (1724–1799)
Reigned in the Electorate of the Palatinate from 1743 and in Palatinate-Bavaria 1777–1799
First marriage in 1742 to Elisabeth Maria Auguste, daughter of the Sulzbach Prince Joseph Karl Emanuel
Second marriage in 1795 to Maria Leopoldine, daughter of Archduke Ferdinand of Austria-Este

ELECTOR MAX IV JOSEPH (FROM THE ZWEIBRÜCKEN-BIRKENFELD LINE, 1756–1825)

Reigned as elector from 1799 and as King Max I Joseph 1806–1825

First marriage in 1785 to Auguste Wilhelmine Maria, daughter of Landgrave Georg Wilhelm of Hessen-Darmstadt

Second marriage in 1797 to Karoline Friederike Wilhelmine, daughter of Prince Karl Ludwig of Baden

King Ludwig I in his coronation robe, Joseph Stieler, 1826, Munich Residence

KING LUDWIG I (1786–1868)

Reigned 1825–1848

Married 1810 to Therese Charlotte Louise, daughter of Duke Friedrich of Sachsen-Hildburghausen

KING MAXIMILIAN II JOSEPH (1811–1864)

Reigned 1848–1864

Married 1842 to Marie Friederike, daughter of Prince Wilhelm of Prussia

KING LUDWIG II (1845–1886)

Reigned 1864–1886

PRINCE REGENT LUITPOLD (1821–1912)

Reigned 1886–1912 (third-oldest son of King Ludwig I)

Married 1844 to Auguste, daughter of Grand Duke Leopold II of Tuscany

KING LUDWIG III (1845–1921)

Reigned as prince regent 1912–1913 and as king 1913–1918

Married 1868 to Maria Therese, daughter of Archduke Ferdinand of Austria-Este

GERECH
UND
BEHARRE

Key dates in the history of Nymphenburg

1663 Kemnath Farm bought for 10,000 florins by Elector Ferdinand Maria for the purpose of building a country residence.

1664 Central pavilion commenced.

1671 First garden behind the palace laid out, with flowerbeds radiating from fountains.

1672 Interior commenced.

1673 H. Zuccalli takes over supervision of the building project. Ceiling paintings in the apartments commenced.

1674 Two side pavilions commenced.

1675 Vaulting of the central hall.

1678 Roof gables taken down and hip roof constructed.

1680 All building work stopped when Max Emanuel comes to power.

1684 Two side pavilions pulled down.

1701 H. Zuccalli and A. Viscardi start extending the palace with two residential pavilions flanking the central building. At the same time Carbonet begins work on an extensive Baroque garden with “Dutch” canals.

1704 Suspension of all building work with the outbreak of the Spanish War of Succession.

1715 Consecration of the Palace Chapel in the second north pavilion. D. Girard from Paris appointed as “fountain master”.

1716 Completion of the second south pavilion (Mundkuchl- und Zergaden-Pavillon).

1716/19 Pagodenburg built by J. Effner. Work on the interior of the main palace.

1716 Orangery building commenced.

1718/21 Badenburg built by J. Effner.

1719 East wing of the southern annex completed, with the elector's stables on the ground floor and cavaliers' rooms on the first floor. Adjoining farm built.

1720/22 Interior of Max Emanuel's apartments on the first floor of the central building and the first north pavilion completed. The North Antechamber, the adjoining Gallery, Max Emanuel's Depeschenkabinett (red Lyons silk wall covering replaced in the original design in 1960/61) and the barrel vaulting of the Antechamber in the north pavilion have all been preserved in their original form.

1723/24 Connecting wing (Passgebäude) built for the Pass-Spiel, a ball game similar to croquet, and billiards; third south building tract also completed, which was fitted out as a kitchen in 1750.

1725/28 Magdalenenklause built by J. Effner.

1728 Crescent ("Rondell") buildings commenced with a pavilion for Court Controller Hieber in the southern section.

1729 Construction of the two crescent buildings next to the palace and the second pavilion in the south section of the crescent for court officials.

1730 Canal built on the town side of the palace, together with the avenues bordered with linden trees leading to the palace. East wing of the northern annex built for nuns from Luxembourg. (This tract was handed over in 1835 to the religious order "Englische Fräulein").

1733 ff. Wall built around the gardens.

1733 ff. North wing of the southern rectangular annex extended to provide new stables.

1734/39 The hunting lodge Amalienburg built by F. Cuvilliés the Elder near the new pheasantry.

1739 Consecration of the chapel built by Effner (destroyed in the Second World War) in the east wing of the northern annex. The original altarpiece (now in the Alte Pinakothek in Munich) had a painting by G.B. Tiepolo of St Clemens, the patron saint of the chapel's founder, Elector Clemens August.

1750 "Former Comedihaus" rebuilt as the "Mundt- und Hofkuchl Building" by J. Gunezrhainer. Electoral farm at Nymphenburg destroyed by lightning and rebuilt.

1755/57 Great Hall in the central building reconstructed by F. Cuvilliés the Elder and J. B. Zimmermann.

1757 Completion of the Aviary in the South Cabinet Garden begun in 1751 by F. Cuvilliés the Elder. Completion of the Orangery tract with the Hubertus Hall in the north side block.

1758 Last pavilion in the crescent completed; in 1761 the Porcelain Manufactory founded by Max III Joseph in Neudeck castle near the river Isar in 1747 is relocated here.

1761 Bernardo Bellotto, known as Canaletto, paints the two famous views of Nymphenburg Palace for the Residence in Munich.

1762 Pump house built between the Amalienburg and the Badenburg to operate the large fountains in the Large Parterre and supply the palace with water. This "Green Pump House" was rebuilt in 1803 for the waterworks designed by J. Baader.

1763/64 Alteration of the two corner cabinets in the central building and other interior renovation work under the supervision of F. Cuvilliés the Elder.

1764 South Cabinet Garden acquires a cascade and fountain designed by F. Cuvilliés the Elder.

1769 Cascade at the west end of the gardens faced in marble. Elector commissions white marble statues of gods for the Large Parterre.

1777/78 Conversion of the upper floor of the court kitchen building into a dining hall ("Green Hall") for the cavaliers.

1778 Reserve for golden pheasants laid out at the edge of the southern half of the park.

1778 Three groups of putti by D. Auliczek erected near the Badenburg. The groups, designed for Elector Max III Joseph as symbols of the three patrons, were placed in front of the palace in the early 19th century (today replaced by copies by J. Enderle, 1918; the originals are in the Orangery building).

1791 Golden pheasant reserve turned into a menagerie building.

1795 The two galleries widened on the garden side with connecting rooms and cabinets.

1799 ff. Wooden summerhouse with the Crown Prince Garden built for Crown Prince Ludwig.

1804/23 F. L. v. Sckell transforms the Baroque garden into an English landscape garden.

1806/08 Rebuilding and redecoration of some of the suites and apartments in the main palace.

1807/08 Pumps in the Johannis Tower of the Orangery built by J. Baader for the fountains on the town side.

1807 ff. Building of the first glasshouse north of the Large Parterre and renovation of the Small Parterre in front of it from designs by F. L. von Sckell.

1815/16 P. Lamine's statue of a flute-playing Pan and a goat is erected in the southern half of the park.

1816 and 1820 Two more glasshouses are built from plans by v. Sckell. Sculpture of a putto riding on a dolphin in the fountain of the parterre in front by J. N. Haller, 1818. Four mythological figures (Judgement of Paris) by L. Ohnmacht (1804/07) arranged by v. Sckell in front of a semicircle of trees.

Around 1820 Neoclassical architecture (Venus by A. Canova and mythological figures by K. Eberhard) added as a backdrop to the cascade of the South Cabinet Garden, which has been transformed in the English style.

1826 Gables at the top of the central building removed and replaced with a wooden cornice by L.v. Klenze.

1835 Renovation of the large waterworks for the fountains on the town side – still in existence – in the well house of the northern side annex.

1865 Monopteros built for King Ludwig I from plans by Klenze as a monument to the creation of the Nymphenburg gardens.

1938 Rebuilding of the Orangery tract, completion of the rear sections of the building.

1944 War damage to the north tract and the Badenburg.

1950 The Marstallmuseum (with the contents of the former court coach-house in the Residence Palace) is established in the former electoral stables in the southern annex.

1952/53 Restoration of the Badenburg and the Magdalenenklause.

1953/56 Renovation of the façades of the main building.

1956/58 Renovation of the Amalienburg.

1959/60 Renovation of the former apartment of Queen Karoline on the first floor of the first south pavilion with the room where King Ludwig II was born, the Study and the Audience Chamber (here primarily reproduction of the brocaded silk coverings in their original form).

1966/67 Restoration of the second South Antechamber and furnishing of the three rooms next to the North Gallery.

1970/72 Restoration of the façades of the main buildings in their original colours – grey-green on white – on the basis of remaining traces of paint, the veduttas of F. J. Beich (1723) in Nymphenburg and the views by Canaletto (Residence Palace).

1974 ff. Restoration of the marble figures. Renovation of the façades of the Orangery tract. Renovation of the interior of the Northern Cavaliers' Building (Marstallmuseum).

1985 Completion of the comprehensive renovation and restoration of the Badenburg begun in 1978.

1985/86 Thorough restoration of the Pagodenburg and Amalienburg façades.

1986 Completion of the renovation of the Northern Cavaliers' Building begun in 1974. Rearrangement and extension of the Marstallmuseum and opening of the Museum of Nymphenburg Porcelain (Bäuml Collection) in the same tract.

1987/89 Rebuilding of the west and south-west wing adjoining the Marstallmuseum on the basis of the Baroque layout with workshops and offices for the Bavarian Palace Department.

1989 Completion of the renovation and restoration of the "Prince's Pavilion".

1990/95 Restoration work in the Great Hall of the main palace. General renovation of the two south pavilions.

1991 Completion of the Palace Chapel restoration begun in 1987.

1993 ff. Renovation of the park wall.

2003 Opening of the restored Karl Theodor Rooms.

2003 Completion of the Orangery tract renovation and opening of the Hubertus Hall as a concert and event room.

2004 Completion of comprehensive renovation of the Pagodenburg.

2007/08 Restoration of the Singerie Cabinet in the Badenburg. Restoration of the Northern Gallery of the central building.

2008 Opening of the museum shop on the ground floor of the central building.

Nymphenburg Palace, Orangery building, Hubertus Hall

Bibliography

OSWALD GÖTZ: Die Amalienburg im Nymphenburger Schloßpark; in: Städel Jahrbuch 2, 1922 pp. 97–108.

LUISA HAGER UND HEINRICH KREISEL: Nymphenburg, Schloß, Park und Burgen, Amtlicher Führer, Munich 1938 ff.

HEINRICH KREISEL: Die Kunstschreiner der Schloßeinrichtungen des Kurfürsten Max III. Joseph von Bayern im späten Rokoko; in: Münchner Jahrbuch, N. F. 1938/39, vol. XIII.

HEINRICH KREISEL: Farbiges Nymphenburg, Munich 1944.

Adalbert Prinz von Bayern, Nymphenburg und seine Bewohner, Munich 1950.

LUISA HAGER: Instandgesetzte Stuckdecken in Schloß Nymphenburg und ihre Meister; in: Deutsche Kunst- und Denkmalpflege, 1953.

LUISA HAGER: Nymphenburg, Schloß, Park und Burgen, Munich 1955 (with detailed bibliography).

HEINRICH KREISEL: Die Instandsetzung der Amalienburg; in: Deutsche Kunst- und Denkmalpflege, 1960.

CHRISTINA THON: Johann Baptist Zimmermann als Stukkator, doctoral dissertation, Mainz 1965, MS.

PETER VOLK: Zur Geschichte der Nymphenburger Gartenplastik 1716–1770; in: Münch. Jahrb. d. bild. Kunst. 3. F., vol. 18, 1967, pp. 211–240.

L. FRHR. VON GUMPPENBERG: Die Amalienburg im Park von Nymphenburg; in: Der Deutsche Jäger, 86th year, April 1968.

LEONORE BERGHOFF, Emanuele Tesauro und seine Concetti, unter besonderer Berücksichtigung von Schloß Nymphenburg, doctoral dissertation, Munich 1971, MS.

HEIDI BÜRKLIN: Franz Joachim Beich (1665–1748). Ein Landschafts- und Schlachtenmaler am Hofe Max Emanuels. Munich 1971 (= Neue Schriftenreihe des Stadtarchivs München vol. 56).

GERHARD HOJER: Die Baugeschichte des Schlosses Nymphenburg; in: Fee Schlapper u.a., Schloß Nymphenburg, Munich 1972, pp. 108–116.

MICHAEL PETZET: Entwürfe für Schloß Nymphenburg; in: Zwischen Donau und Alpen, Festschrift N. Lieb, Munich 1972, pp. 202–212.

PETER VIERL: Die Erneuerung der Schloßfassaden von Nymphenburg. Ein Beitrag zur Putz- und Stucktechnik in der Denkmalpflege; in: Maltechnik-Restauro 1972, no. 1, pp. 36–39; no. 2, pp. 100–104; no. 3, pp. 205–210.

PETER VIERL: Die Putz- und Anstricherneuerung bei der Fassadeninstandsetzung am Schloß Nymphenburg; in: Deutsche Kunst- und Denkmalpflege 1972, pp. 43–48.

LISELOTTE ANDERSEN: Eine unbekannte Quellenschrift aus der Zeit um 1700; in: Münch. Jahrb. d. bild. Kunst, 3. F. vol. 24, 1973, pp. 175–237.

GISELA VITS: Joseph Effners Palais Preysing. Ein Beitrag zur Münchener Profanarchitektur des Spätbarock, Frankfurt/M. 1973 (= Kieler Kunsthistor. Studien vol. 5).

PETER VIERL: Neue Erkenntnisse zur Baugeschichte des Schlosses Nymphenburg; in: Jahrbuch der Bayerischen Denkmalpflege vol. 29, 1972–74, pp. 97–115.

JOHANN GEORG PRINZ VON HOHENZOLLERN: Peter Jakob Horemans (1700–1776). Exhibition catalogue, Munich 1974.

Kurfürst Max Emanuel. Bayern und Europa um 1700 (exhibition catalogue), vols. 1 and 2, Munich 1976.

ELMAR D. SCHMID: Nymphenburg. Schloß und Garten, Pagodenburg, Badenburg, Magdalenenklause, Amalienburg, Munich 1979.

(exhibition catalogue) Wittelsbach und Bayern III., vols. 1 and 2, Munich 1980.

(exhibition catalogue) Klassizismus in Bayern, Schwaben und Franken, Munich 1980.

ULRIKA KIBY-RATKA: Die Küche der Amalienburg im Schloßgarten von Nymphenburg zu München, Heidelberg 1981.

ELMAR D. SCHMID: Eine unbekannte Ansicht der Magdalenenklause im Schloßpark zu Nymphenburg; in: Weltkunst year 51, 1981, no. 13, pp. 1959–1961.

ELMAR D. SCHMID: Bemerkungen zur Restaurierung der Badenburg im Park von Schloß Nymphenburg; in: Ars Bavarica vol. 31/32, 1983, pp. 89–96.

FRIEDERIKE WAPPENSCHMIDT: »Indianische Tapezereyen« in den Münchner Schlössern des 18. Jahrhunderts; in: Ars Bavarica vol. 31/32, 1983, pp. 97–120 (Restaurierungsbericht von M. Heise, pp. 121–124).

SABINE HEYM: Henrico Zuccalli (um 1642–1724). Der kurbayerische Hofbaumeister, Munich and Zürich 1984.

DIETRICH VON FRANK: Joseph Effners Pagodenburg. Studien zu einer »maison de plaisance«, Munich 1985.

UTA SCHEDLER: Roman Anton Boos (1733–1810). Bildhauer zwischen Rokoko und Klassizismus, Munich and Zürich 1985.

ANNA BAUER-WILD: Die erste Bau- und Ausstattungsphase des Schlosses Nymphenburg (1663–1680), Munich 1986.

WOLFGANG BRAUNFELS: François Cuvilliés. Der Baumeister der galanten Architektur des Rokoko, Munich 1986.

GESCHE VON DEESEN: Die Badenburg im Park von Nymphenburg, Munich 1986.

GERHARD HOJER: Die Amalienburg. Rokokojuwel im Nymphenburger Schloßpark, Munich and Zürich 1986.

ELMAR D. SCHMID AND SABINE HEYM: Joseph Effner 1687–1745. Bauten für Kurfürst Max Emanuel. Exhibition texts, Dachau 1987.

ELLIS KAUT: Der Nymphenburger Park, Munich 1987 (picture book).

HERMANN BAUER AND BERNHARD RUPPRECHT: Corpus der barocken Deckenmalerei in Deutschland, vol. 3, part 2, Munich 1989.

DIETRICH VON FRANK: Die »maison de plaisance«. Ihre Entwicklung in Frankreich und Rezeption in Deutschland, Munich 1989.

HORST MELLENTHIN: François Cuvilliés' Amalienburg. Ihr Bezug zur französischen Architekturtheorie, Munich 1989.

FRIEDERIKE WAPPENSCHMIDT: Chinesische Tapeten für Europa. Vom Rollenbild zur Bildtapete, Berlin 1989.

ULRIKA KIBY: Die Exotismen des Kurfürsten Max Emanuel in Nymphenburg, Hildesheim, Zürich, New York 1990.

NIKOLENKO LADA: Schönheitsgalerien der Wittelsbacher, Munich 1990.

HILDEGARD MERZENICH: Das Nymphenburger Schloßrondell. Mittelpunkt und Denkmal eines Idealstadt-Konzepts; in: Schönere Heimat year 79, 1990, no. 4, pp. 235–240.

KAI UWE NIELSEN: Die Magdalenenklause im Schloßpark zu Nymphenburg, Munich 1990.

UTA SCHEDLER: Die Statuenzyklen in den Schloßgärten von Schönbrunn und Nymphenburg, Hildesheim, Zürich, New York 1990.

FRIEDERIKE WAPPENSCHMIDT: Der Traum von Arkadien. Leben, Liebe, Licht und Farbe in Europas Lustschlössern, Munich 1990.

BRIGITTE LANGER: Die Möbel der Residenz München. I. Die französischen Möbel des 18. Jahrhunderts, Munich 1995.

BRIGITTE LANGER, ALEXANDER HERZOG VON WÜRTTEMBERG: Die Möbel der Residenz München. II. Die deutschen Möbel des 16.–18. Jahrhunderts, Munich 1996.

ANNA BAUER-WILD: Ergänzungen zur Baugeschichte Nymphenburgs unter Max Emanuel 1701–04. In: Monumental: Festschrift für Michael Petzet zum 65. Geburtstag am 12. April 1998. Susanne Böning-Weis, Karlheinz Hemmeter, York Langenstein (eds) (Arbeitshefte des Bayerischen Landesamtes für Denkmalpflege, vol. 100), Munich 1998, pp. 564–579.

BRIGITTE LANGER: Die Möbel der Schlösser Nymphenburg und Schleißheim, Munich, London, New York 2000.

NORBERT HIERL-DERONCO: Es ist eine Lust zu bauen. Von Bauherren, Bauleuten und vom Bauen im Barock in Kurbayern – Franken – Rheinland, Krailling 2001.

ERNST GÖTZ: Französische Schmiedekunst an deutschen Schlössern. Der Kunstschlosser Antoine Motté am kurbayerischen Hof. In: ARX, Burgen und Schlösser in Bayern, Österreich und Südtirol, no. 2, 2002, pp. 35–41.

MAX TILLMANN: Ein Frankreichbündnis der Kunst. Kurfürst Max Emanuel von Bayern als Auftraggeber und Sammler. Deutsches Forum für Kunstgeschichte (ed) (passages vol. 25), Munich 2009.

Index of artists and artisans

Plan of the Nymphenburg Palace Park

1 Cour d'honneur with fountain
2 Main Palace with ticket office and shop
3 Palace Chapel
4 "Mensch und Natur" Museum
5 Orangery tract with Hubertus Hall
6 Johannis Tower with historic pump system
7 Nymphenburg Porcelain Manufactory
8 Erwin von Kreibig Museum
9 Marstallmuseum with the Nymphenburg Porcelain Museum
10 Bavarian Department for State-owned Palaces, Gardens and Lakes
11 Large Parterre with fountain
12 South Cabinet Garden*
13 Crown Prince Garden with pavilion
14 Amalienburg
15 Former Menagerie*
16 Little Village with "Green Pump House" open from Easter to the beginning of October 9am – 4pm
17 Pan Statue with spring
18 Badenburg
19 Lion Valley ("Löwental")
20 Badenburg Lake
21 Monopteros
22 Southern vista
23 Large Cascade
24 Central canal
25 Northern vista
26 Pagodenburg Lake
27 Pagodenburg
28 Pagodenburg Valley with "Kugelweiher"
29 Former farm*
30 Magdalenenklause
31 Historic glass-houses and exhibition "Friedrich Ludwig von Sckell and Nymphenburg. The history, design and maintenance of the palace park". Open from the beginning of April to mid-October 9am – 6pm
32 North Cabinet Garden*
33 Nursery with historic green-house*
34 Passage to Botanical Gardens (open from April to September)
35 Ha-has in the park wall

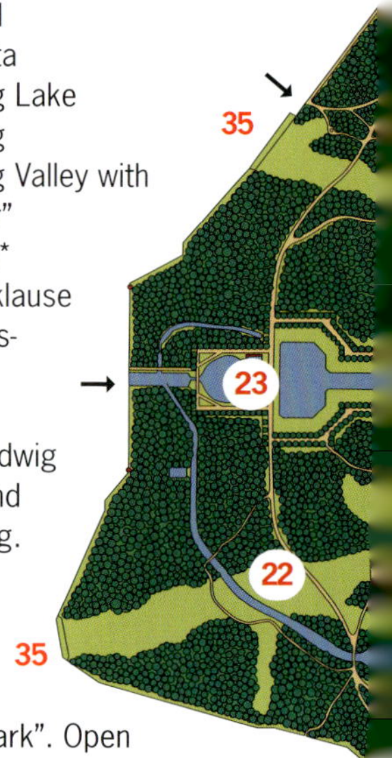

* not accessible
→ park gates

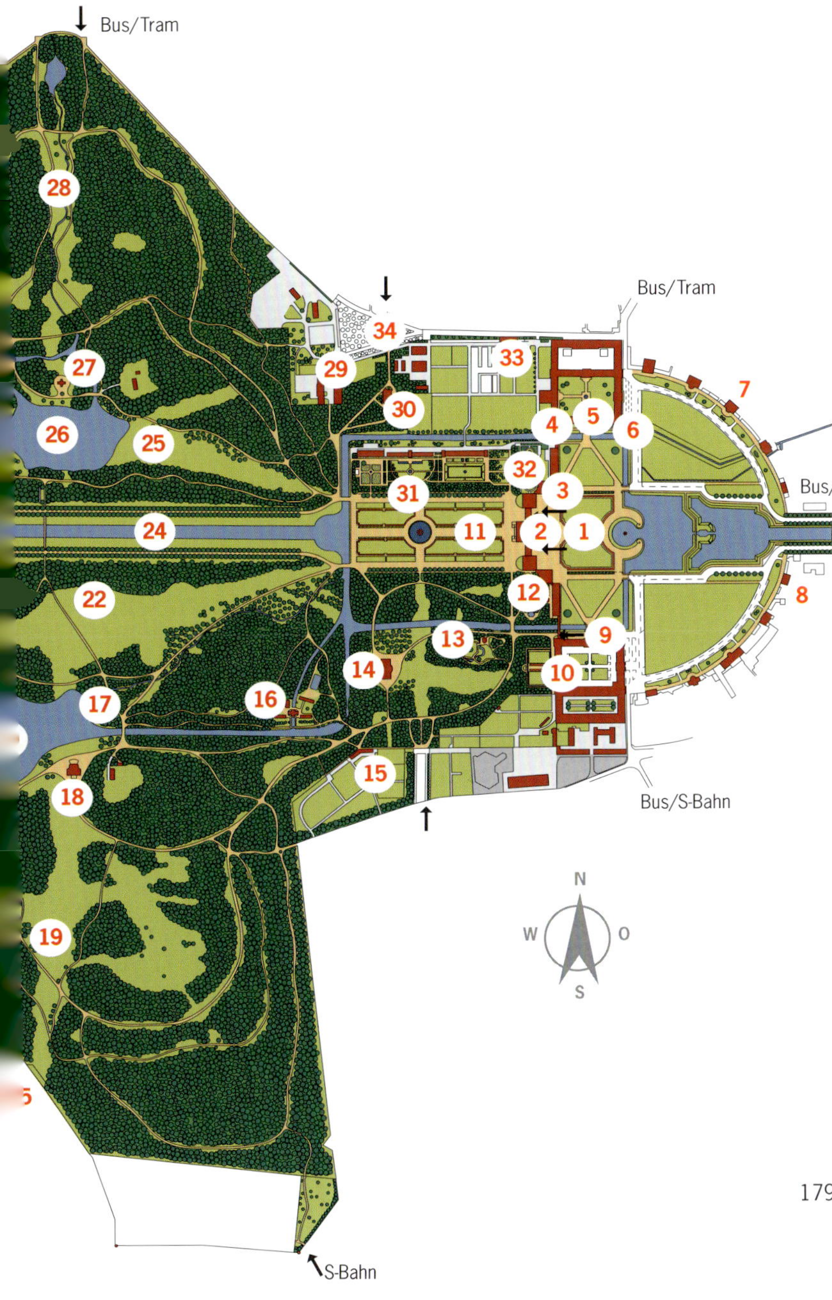
Bus/Tram
Bus/Tram
Bus/Tram
Bus/S-Bahn
S-Bahn
N
W
O
S
1
2
3
4
5
6
7
8
9
10
11
12
13
14
15
16
17
18
19
22
24
25
26
27
28
29
30
31
32
33
34

PLACES OF INTEREST ADMINISTERED BY THE BAVARIAN PALACE DEPARTMENT

www.schloesser.bayern.de

Ansbach ■ **Residence of the Margraves of Ansbach**
Early Rococo state apartments, collection of Ansbach faience and porcelain, Court Garden with orangery
TEL. (09 81) 95 38 39-0 · **FAX** (09 81) 95 38 39-40

Aschaffenburg ■ **Johannisburg Palace**
Art gallery and electoral apartments, collection of cork models, Palace Garden, Municipal Palace Museum
TEL. (0 60 21) 3 86 57-0 · **FAX** (0 60 21) 3 86 57-16

■ **Pompeiianum**
Replica of a Roman villa and Antiquities Museum

■ **Schönbusch Palace and Park**
Small Neoclassical palace in an English landscape garden

Bamberg ■ **New Residence in Bamberg**
Imperial Hall and Baroque state rooms, art gallery, Rose Garden
TEL. (09 51) 5 19 39-0 und 5 19 39-1 14 · **FAX** (09 51) 5 19 39-1 29

Bamberg/ Memmelsdorf ■ **Seehof Palace**
Residential and state rooms, Rococo garden, cascade with waterworks
TEL. (09 51) 40 95-70 · **FAX** (09 51) 40 95-72

Bayreuth ■ **New Palace**
Margravial residence in the Bayreuth Rococo style with the Wilhelmine Museum, the Museum of Bayreuth Faience, Court Garden with orangery
TEL. (09 21) 7 59 69-0 · **FAX** (09 21) 7 59 69-15

■ **Margravial Opera House**

Bayreuth/ Donndorf ■ **Museum of Garden Design Fantaisie Palace and Park**
TEL. (09 21) 73 14 00-11 · **FAX** (09 21) 73 14 00-18

Bayreuth/ Hermitage ■ **Hermitage Old Palace**
Margravine Wilhelmine's rooms, grotto, historic gardens with waterworks
TEL. (09 21) 7 59 69-37· **FAX** (09 21) 7 59 69-87

Bayr./Wonsees Sanspareil ■ **Rock Garden and Oriental Building**
Rococo rooms, garden parterre and Rock Garden
TEL. (0 92 74) 9 09 89-06 · **FAX** (0 92 74) 9 09 89-07

■ **Zwernitz Castle** · Castle complex

Burg Lauenstein
Ludwigsstadt
72
Schloss Rosenau
Coburg
Veste Coburg
Schloss Ehrenburg
Kulmbach
Plassenburg
7
Burg Zwernitz
Felsengarten Sanspareil
70
Neue Residenz Bamberg
Schloss Seehof
Bayreuth
Schloss Eremitage
Markgräfliches Opernhaus
Johannisburg
Würzburg
Schloss Veitshöchheim
Residenz Würzburg
Alte Hof-haltung
Bamberg
Schloss Fantaisie
Neues Schloss Bayreuth
3
Festung Marienberg
73
9
Schnaittach
Festung Rothenberg
Cadolzburg
Nürnberg
Tucherschlösschen
93
7
Residenz Ansbach
Kaiserburg Nürnberg
6
Ansbach
6
3
Residenz Ellingen
Weissenburg
Regensburg
Riedenburg
Eichstätt
Rosenburg
Befreiungshalle Kelheim
Kelheim
3
Burg Prunn
Willibaldsburg
93
Schloss Neuburg
Neuburg
92
Dillingen
Schloss Höchstädt
Landshut
Stadtresidenz Landshut
Burg Trausnitz
9
8
Neu-Ulm
Augsburg
Schloss Dachau
Schloss Lustheim
Schloss Schleißheim
Burg Burghausen
7
Englischer Garten
Schloss Nymphenburg
Residenz München
Ruhmeshalle und Bavaria
München
96
Künstlerhaus Gasteiger
Ammersee
Chiem-see
Schloss Herrenchiemsee
Roseninsel Park Feldafing
Starnberger See
8
Residenz Kempten
95
Künstlerhaus Exter
Kempten
Staffel-see
Tegern-see
93
Forggen-see
Bodensee
Schloss Linderhof
Lindau
Ettal
St. Bartholomä
Füssen
Garmisch-Partenkirchen
Königs-see
Schloss Neuschwanstein
Königshaus am Schachen

Burghausen ■ **Burghausen Castle**
Castle complex, ducal apartments, chapel, State Gallery of Old German Masters and Historical Paintings, viewing platform
TEL. (0 86 77) 46 59 · **FAX** (0 86 77) 6 56 74

Cadolzburg ■ **Castle and Castle Garden**
TEL. (09 11) 24 46 59-0 · **FAX** (09 11) 24 46 59-300

Coburg ■ **Ehrenburg Palace**
Historical residential and state rooms from the Baroque era and the 19th century
TEL. (0 95 61) 80 88-32 · **FAX** (0 95 61) 80 88-31

Coburg/ Rödental ■ **Rosenau Palace**
Set in an English landscape garden; residential rooms from the Biedermeier period and Neo-Gothic Marble Hall
TEL. (0 95 63) 30 84-10 · **FAX** (0 95 61) 30 84-29

Dachau ■ **Dachau Palace**
Hall, staircase, Court Garden
TEL. (0 81 31) 8 79 23 · **FAX** (0 81 31) 7 85 73

Eichstätt ■ **Willibaldsburg**
Fortress complex, Jura Museum, Prehistoric and Early History Museum, Bastion Garden
TEL. (0 84 21) 47 30 · **FAX** (0 84 21) 81 94

Ellingen ■ **Ellingen Residence**
The state apartments of Prince von Wrede, rooms of the Deutscher Orden, palace church, historical park
TEL. (0 91 41) 9 74 79-0 · **FAX** (0 91 41) 9 74 79-7

Feldafing am Starnberger See ■ **Feldafing Park and Rose Island**
TEL. (0 81 51) 69 75 · **FAX** (0 81 51) 36 81 23

Herrenchiemsee ■ **Herrenchiemsee New Palace**
Residential and state rooms, historical gardens with waterworks and **King Ludwig II Museum**
TEL. (0 80 51) 68 87-0 · **FAX** (0 80 51) 68 87-99

■ **Museum in the Augustinian monastery Herrenchiemsee (Old Palace)**
Permanent exhibition on the former monastery and the constitutional convention, State Rooms in the Princes' Tract, apartment of King Ludwig II; Julius Exter Art Gallery; Maler am Chiemsee Gallery

Höchstädt ■ **Höchstädt Palace**
Exhibition on the Battle of Höchstädt/Blenheim 1704, Chapel, Museum of German Faience
TEL. (0 90 74) 95 85-7 12 · **FAX** (0 90 74) 95 85-7 91

Holzhausen ■ **Gasteiger House**
Collection of Anna and Mathias Gasteiger's works in the rooms of the summer villa where they lived, landscape garden
TEL. (0 88 06) 6 99

Kelheim ■ **Hall of Liberation**
Neoclassical memorial, impressive domed hall, view of the surroundings from the open gallery
TEL. (0 94 41) 6 82 07-10 · **FAX** (0 94 41) 6 82 07-20

Kempten ■ **Kempten Residence**
State rooms and Throne Room of the prince-abbots
TEL. (08 31) 2 56-2 51 · **FAX** (08 31) 2 56-2 60

Königssee ■ **St. Bartholomä**
St. Bartholomä Church, hunting lodge, chapel of St Johann and St Paul, Berchtesgaden national park
TEL. (0 80 51) 9 66 58-0 · **FAX** (0 80 51) 9 66 58-38

Kulmbach ■ **Plassenburg**
Schöner Hof (Beautiful Courtyard), Hohenzollern Museum, »Frederick the Great« Army Museum
TEL. (0 92 21) 82 20-0 · **FAX** (0 92 21) 82 20-26

Landshut ■ **Trausnitz Castle**
Castle complex, medieval halls and castle chapel, Fools' Staircase, Renaissance rooms, Museum of Renaissance Art
TEL. (08 71) 9 24 11-0/-44 · **FAX** (08 71) 9 24 11-40

■ **Town Residence**
First palace in Italian Renaissance style north of the Alps; Neoclassical Birkenfeld Rooms

Lauenstein near Ludwigsstadt ■ **Lauenstein Castle**
Castle complex, residential rooms, special museum collections
TEL. (0 92 63) 4 00 · **FAX** (0 92 63) 97 44 22

Linderhof ■ **Linderhof Palace**
Residential and state rooms, Venus Grotto, Moroccan House, Moorish Kiosk, Hunding's Hut and the Hermitage of Gurnemanz, historic gardens with waterworks
TEL. (0 88 22) 92 03-0 · **FAX** (0 88 22) 92 03-11

Munich ■ **Munich Residence and Court Garden**
Historical residential and state rooms representing a range of epochs from the Renaissance to the 19th century, court church and chapel, special collections (silver, porcelain, sacred vestments, reliquaries)
TEL. (0 89) 2 90 67-1 · **FAX** (0 89) 2 90 67-2 25

Treasury of the Residence

Cuvilliés Theatre

■ **Feldherrnhalle (Field Marshals' Hall)**

■ **Hall of Fame and statue of Bavaria**
on the Theresienhöhe

■ **Nymphenburg Palace**
State rooms, Great Hall, Gallery of Beauties, palace chapel
TEL. (0 89) 1 79 08-0 · **FAX** (0 89) 1 79 08-6 27

Amalienburg, Badenburg, Pagodenburg, Magdalenenklause
in the historical palace park

Marstallmuseum
Court carriages and sleighs, saddles and other riding equipment

Museum of Nymphenburg Porcelain
Bäuml Collection

■ **English Garden**
Landscape garden in the English style
TEL. (0 89) 3 86 66 39-0 · **FAX** (0 89) 3 86 66 39-23

Munich/ Oberschleißheim ■ **Schleißheim New Palace**
Halls, state apartments, art gallery, Baroque Court Garden
TEL. (0 89) 31 58 72-0 · **FAX** (0 89) 31 58 72-50

■ **Lustheim Palace**
Museum of Meißen Porcelain, hall

Neuburg a.d. Donau ■ **Neuburg Palace on the Danube**
Sgraffito façade, 1st Protestant chapel, grottoes, Pfalz-Neuburg Museum, Museum of Baroque sacred art, Museum of Archaeology, State Gallery of Flemish Art
TEL. (0 84 31) 64 43-0 · **FAX** (0 84 31) 64 43-44

Neuschwanstein/ Schwangau ■ **Neuschwanstein Castle**
Royal apartments and state rooms
TEL. (0 83 62) 9 39 88-0 · **FAX** (0 83 62) 9 39 88-19

Nuremberg ■ **Imperial Castle of Nuremberg**
Palas, period rooms, double chapel, Deep Well and Sinwell Tower, Castle Gardens
TEL. (09 11) 24 46 59-0 · **FAX** (09 11) 24 46 59-300

Prunn im Altmühltal ■ **Prunn Castle**
Historical castle rooms, chapel
TEL. (0 94 42) 33 23 · **FAX** (0 94 42) 33 35

Riedenburg ■ **Rosenburg Castle**
Castle complex with a privately run falconry
TEL. (0 94 42) 27 52 · **FAX** (0 94 42) 32 87

Schachen ■ **King's House on the Schachen**
Residential rooms and Turkish Hall, alpine garden
TEL. (0 88 22) 92 03-0 · **FAX** (0 88 22) 92 03-11

Schnaittach ■ **Rothenburg Fortress**
The ruins of an 18th-century fortress complex
TEL. (0 91 53) 80 78 (Heimatverein)

Übersee/ Feldwies ■ **Exter House** with the atelier of the artist Julius Exter
TEL. (0 86 42) 89 50-83 · **FAX** (0 86 42) 89 50-85

Veitshöchheim ■ **Veitshöchheim Palace and Garden**
Historical residential rooms,
Exhibition on the history of the Court Garden,
Rococo Garden with waterworks
TEL. (09 31) 9 15 82

Wonsees ■ See Bayreuth

Würzburg ■ **Würzburg Residence**
Baroque state rooms, frescos by G.B. Tiepolo, art gallery, Court Gardens
TEL. (09 31) 3 55 17-0 · **FAX** (09 31) 3 55 17-25

■ **Marienberg Fortress**
Fortress complex, Prince's Building Museum with Treasury, Sacred Vestment Room and municipal history collections, Maschikuli Tower, Prince's Garden, Main-Franconian Museum

Antiquarium in the Munich Residence

Residence Museum · Treasury Cuvilliés Theatre

From 1508 –1918, the Munich Residence was the seat and centre of government of the Wittelsbach dynasty. With over 130 period rooms from the Renaissance, Baroque, Rococo and Neoclassical epochs and the numerous special collections, it is one of the most important palace museums in Europe. Also in the Residence is the Treasury of the Wittelsbachs with valuable exhibits from nine centuries. The Cuvilliés Theatre is the oldest opera house in Munich and is impressively decorated in the South German Rococo style.

Statuette of St George, Treasury

Auditorium of the Cuvilliés Theatre

Hall of Fame and Bavaria

Hall of Fame and Bavaria

The Hall of Fame and Bavaria were built as a national monument under King Ludwig I of Bavaria. The 18.50-metre-high Bavaria is the first large sculpture of the Modern Period. The statue, which has a staircase inside, was designed by Ludwig Michael von Schwanthaler. In the three-winged Hall of Fame are busts of well-known people who have rendered service to Bavaria.

English Garden

The public gardens in the style of a classical landscape garden were begun in 1789 under Elector Karl Theodor. From 1804, the park was completed under the direction of Friedrich Ludwig Sckell according to the principles of English garden design. The English Garden is of high aesthetic quality and an important landmark in social history as the first public garden on the continent. With its generous dimensions and constantly changing views of park architecture and landscape features, it is a model example of a classical landscape garden.

English Garden in Munich

Rose Island with the villa called the Casino

Rose Island

The idyllic Rose Island with its small island villa, known as the Casino, and its splendid rose garden is one of Lake Starnberg's most delightful features and was a favourite place of King Ludwig II. In around 1850, Ludwig's father, King Maximilian II, had transformed the former fishermen's island of Wörth into a royal refuge full of fragrant roses. A visit to the island, which has an area of 2.5 hectares and is accessed by ferry boat, is an unforgettable experience.

Dachau Palace

Dachau Palace originated as an early medieval castle belonging to the Counts of Dachau. During the reigns of Duke Wilhelm IV and Duke Albrecht V, it was transformed into a massive four-winged palace complex. The tract facing the Court Garden was taken up by the festival hall, with a wooden Renaissance ceiling that is one of the most important of its kind in southern Germany. In 1715, Elector Max Emanuel had the hall tract and its magnificent staircase redesigned in the Baroque style by Joseph Effner. At the beginning of the 19th century three-quarters of the complex was pulled down.

Dachau Palace with Court Garden

Schleißheim New Palace seen from the park

Schleißheim Palace complex

The Schleißheim palace complex is one of the largest and most impressive Wittelsbach residences in Bavaria. The Old Palace was built as a ducal country seat in the early 17th century. The Late Baroque palace buildings from the time of Elector Max Emanuel, the monumental New Palace and the hunting lodge Lustheim, were constructed around what is one of the most important Baroque gardens in Europe. The interior of the festival halls and state apartments, the European Baroque paintings in the New Palace and the collection of early Meissen porcelain in Lustheim Palace are among the best of their era.

New Palace, Sala terrena, grisaille painting by Nikolaus Gottfried Stuber, Ceres as an allegory of summer

Large Gallery

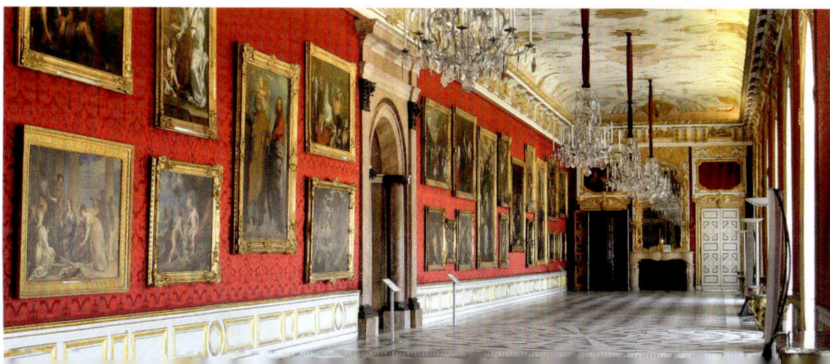

THE PUBLICATIONS OF THE BAVARIAN PALACE DEPARTMENT

The Bavarian Palace Department publishes official guides with colour photos on all the places of interest for which it is responsible; a number of these are available in several languages. It also offers plans of many of the parks accompanied by brief, illustrated descriptions. Exhibition catalogues and inventories, picture books and scientific works complete the varied spectrum of publications. In addition to the books there are also posters, CD-ROMs and videos on individual properties and special topics.

A complete list of publications can be ordered free of charge from the following address:

Bayerische Verwaltung der
staatlichen Schlösser, Gärten und Seen

Postfach 20 20 63 · 80020 München
Fon +49 (0)89 179 08-0 · Fax +49 (0)89 179 08-190
online-bookshop: www.schloesser.bayern.de

OFFICIAL GUIDES

Published in German; some also available in English, French, Italian, Spanish and Japanese

Ansbach	Residenz Ansbach mit Hofgarten und Orangerie
Aschaffenburg	Aschaffenburg Castle; Das Pompejanum in Aschaffenburg (with English summary); Schloss und Park Schönbusch
Bamberg/Memmelsdorf	Neue Residenz Bamberg (with English summary); Schloss und Park Seehof
Bayreuth	The Hermitage at Bayreuth; Markgräfliches Opernhaus Bayreuth (with English summary), Neues Schloss Bayreuth
Bayreuth/Wonsees	Felsengarten Sanspareil, Burg Zwernitz (with English summary)
Burghausen	Burg zu Burghausen (with English summary)
Coburg	Coburg Ehrenburg Palace
Coburg/Rödental	Schloss Rosenau (with English summary)
Dachau	Schloss Dachau
Eichstätt	Willibaldsburg Eichstätt
Ellingen	Residenz Ellingen
Feldafing	Die Roseninsel im Starnberger See
Herrenchiemsee	Augustinian Monastery and New Palace of Herrenchiemsee
Kelheim	Kelheim Hall of Liberation
Königssee	St. Bartholomä am Königssee (with English summary)
Kulmbach	Plassenburg ob Kulmbach
Landshut	Landshut Burg Trausnitz; Stadtresidenz Landshut
Lauenstein b. Ludwigsstadt	Burg Lauenstein
Linderhof	Linderhof Palace
Munich	Residence Munich; The Treasury in the Munich Residence; Altes Residenztheater/Cuvilliés-Theater; Englischer Garten München (with English summary); Ruhmeshalle und Bavaria; Nymphenburg, Palace, Park and Pavilions; Marstallmuseum Schloss Nymphenburg
Neuburg a.d. Donau	Schloss Neuburg a.d. Donau
Neuschwanstein	Neuschwanstein Castle
Nuremberg	Imperial Castle Nuremberg
Oberschleißheim	Schlossanlage Schleißheim (with English summary)
Prunn	Burg Prunn
Riedenburg	Burg Rosenburg in Riedenburg an der Altmühl
Schachen	The Royal House on the Schachen
Veitshöchheim	Schloss und Hofgarten Veitshöchheim
Würzburg	Festung Marienberg zu Würzburg; The Würzburg Residence and Court Gardens

The present official guide is based on the 1999 edition, but has been fully revised.
Revision and picture editing by Max Tillmann.
Revised by Brigitte Langer

Picture credits:
Artothek/Bayer&Mitko für Bayerische Staatsgemäldesammlungen, München: S. 13

Bayerische Schlösserverwaltung, München: U1, S. 3, 6, 11, 12 (Leihgabe Bayer. Staatsgemäldesammlungen), 16, 19, 21, 24, 29, 31, 34–35, 37, 39, 42–43, 44–45, 46, 52, 53, 55, 57, 58, 59, 61, 62, 64–65, 67, 68, 69, 70, 74, 77, 78, 81, 83, 85, 86, 87, 88, 91, 92–93, 94, 97, 101, 102, 103, 104, 105, 107, 108, 110–111, 113, 114, 117, 118, 120–121, 123, 124, 127, 131, 133, 134, 137, 138, 140, 141, 142, 143, 145, 146, 148, 149, 150, 151, 154, 156, 157, 158, 161, 169, 186, 187, 188, 189, 190, U4 (Fotos: Andrea Gruber/Rainer Herrmann/Ulrich Pfeuffer/Maria Scherf/Markus Traub/L.Weiss u. a.); S. 49, 50 (Fotos: Achim Bunz, München); S. 109 (Foto: Rainer Herzog); S. 54, 72, 130 (Fotos: Philipp Mansmann); S. 98, 153 (Fotos: Elmar D. Schmid)

Bibliothèque de l'Institut de France: S. 14–15

Helicolor Luftbild GmbH: S. 4–5

Münchner Stadtmuseum: S. 40

Konrad Rainer, Salzburg: S. 8–9, 71, 84

Günther Schmid, München: S. 22, 32

Staatliche Graphische Sammlung, München, Inv.- Nr. 46922 Z: S. 26–27

Plan of the palace and park: Norbert Nordmann

Index of artists and artisans: Irmgard Killing

1st edition of the new version

Project manager: Kathrin Jung
Translated by Sue Bollans
Edited by Irmgard Killing
Layout, typography and setting: Barbara Markwitz, Munich
Lithography: Reproline Genceller, Munich
Printed by Sellier Druck, Freising
ISBN 978-3-932982-95-8
Printed in Germany